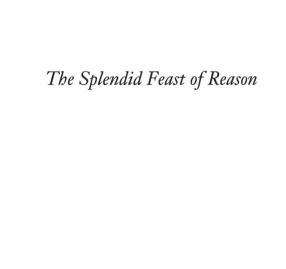

The Splendid Feast of Reason

The Splendid Feast of Reason

S. Jonathan Singer

UNIVERSITY OF CALIFORNIA PRESS

Berkeley   Los Angeles   London

570·1
S6175

University of California Press
Berkeley and Los Angeles, California

University of California Press, Ltd.
London, England

pv/

© 2001 by the Regents of the University of California

Library of Congress Cataloging-in-Publication Data

Singer, Seymour Jonathan, 1924–

    The splendid feast of reason / S. Jonathan Singer.
        p.   cm.
    Includes bibliographical references and index.
    ISBN 0-520-22425-6 (cloth : alk. paper)
      1. Life sciences—Philosophy.   2. Rationalism.
    3. Science—Philosophy.   I. Title.
    QH331.S47   2001
    570'.1—dc21   00-069957

Manufactured in the United States of America
10   09   08   07   06   05   04   03   02   01
10   9   8   7   6   5   4   3   2   1

To Present and Future Young Rationalists

Awake my S. Jon! leave all meaner things
To low ambition and would-be science kings.

(With apologies to Alexander Pope)

The only good is knowledge, the only evil, ignorance.

Socrates

I do not propose to write an ode to dejection,
but to brag as lustily as chanticleer in the morning,
standing on his roost, if only to wake my neighbors up.

Henry David Thoreau

CONTENTS

PREFACE

When I have to decide whether or not to read a book, I first like to know a few things about the author. Why should I relinquish some of my precious time and dwindling span of attention to this one out of the profusion of books competing for my notice and respect, not to mention my cash? Now, I don't care whether an author is a wine aficionado, or makes a mean Creole gumbo, but I do need to know where he or she is coming from and what the true agenda of the book might be. How have personal background and experiences qualified the author to write, shall we say, authoritatively on the subject at hand? What driving force has inspired the writer to undertake the presumptuous task of committing his or her opinions and convictions to indelible print? Assuming that my readers have similar needs, I will now attempt to help them decide whether to go on reading.

I have been a research scientist and university teacher for most of my life, my scientific interests having focused on the borderline between chemistry and biology—the chemistry of life. For a long time, I have been a card-carrying molecular and cell biologist. These facts are especially relevant to this book because an understanding of modern biology is the strongest of the threads binding the book together. Remarkable new information and insight into the deepest nature of life have been obtained by molecular and cell biologists at an ever-increasing pace in the past 50 years. The nature and significance of this knowledge are not yet widely appreciated in the society at large, which is still uneasy about accepting the 150-year-old tenets of Darwinian evolution. Even scientists who are not modern biologists are generally only superficially aware of these more recent revolutionary developments.

Molecular and cell biologists are continually confronted in their studies with the material properties of life, how the chemical substances that make up living systems carry out their many operations. This materialistic outlook gives them no pause about the profoundly radical nature of their pursuits, one of which is biology's Holy Grail, the origin of life. Almost all molecular biologists now take for granted that life on Earth began spontaneously some 4 billion years ago solely by the inevitable action of chemical and physical forces and that it then evolved slowly but inexorably over time to its present spectacular state. Their work also cultivates in biologists a deep appreciation that our genes have an enormous influence on human life and behavior, a view that others in society are largely indisposed to accept. Having lived through and participated in this revolution from its beginnings, I have made these and related facts and ideas the sinews of this book.

For about 40 years, or until about 15 years ago, I was completely absorbed in my professional career. To be sure, I enjoyed my family, applauded the occasional string quartet, booed a baseball umpire once in a while, and was socially and politically conscious, if not active. But looking back on that time, I realize that science was my one consuming passion. As often happens when scientists become "mature," however, around the age of 60, I began for the first time to think seriously about things beyond the classroom and laboratory. From having been only casually conscious of the human condition, I became keenly interested in trying to understand it. Because my predilections were still scientific, I wanted particularly to explore what the new knowledge of biology and the other sciences might contribute to my comprehension of the world and its affairs.

What I have to write next is, unfortunately, not easy for me to convey. Opening my eyes and mind to the human condition was shattering. I experienced something close to Sara Teasdale's vision:

When I can look Life in the eyes,
Grown calm and very coldly wise,
Life will have given me the Truth,
And taken in exchange—my youth.

To my utter dismay, the inattentive unworldliness that had allowed my life its undeflected momentum vanished. I comprehended for the first time what the Preacher meant when he wrote, "He who increaseth knowledge increaseth sorrow." When I was much younger and joyfully dedicated to the pursuit of scientific knowledge, this aphorism did not make any sense to me. What I later came to understand about the human predicament, however, confirmed this ancient prophecy. The more I came to understand, the unhappier I became.

Life in Western society has become amazingly complicated and unmanageable, particularly in the past few hundred years. An unsparing view of our present condition is that we are heading for disaster unless much higher levels of intelligence and altruism are applied to our burgeoning problems, levels that well exceed what most human beings appear to be genetically capable of achieving. Wisdom, alas, consists in realizing that most people haven't a clue about the direction of the lives they lead, let alone about the supervision and control of the complex world around them. This idea is by no means mine alone; it is the unutterable and lacerating view of many intelligent people, who naturally find there is no profit in proclaiming it. This knowledge has not given me perverse pleasure, nor has it fueled a Nietzschean rage against my fellow human beings. What would be the point to that, when most of them, after all, are benighted victims rather than malevolent victimizers? (In this richest democracy on earth, fully one-third of our children live in households with incomes near or below the poverty level. One-fourth of all black youths have been, or are now, in prison. For most of the society, however, these intolerable statistics have about the same reality as UFO sightings. The solutions of society's leaders? Simple. Gut the welfare program, substituting for it a virtual, largely dysfunctional, workfare scheme; reduce taxes on the well-to-do so that they can buy their third Mercedes; and, of course, build more prisons.)

Instead of responding with cynicism or rage, and since I could not ignore or forget what I had learned, I tried to accept and internalize that wisdom and come to live with it. Having been a teacher for most of my life, I was in any event not about to broadcast my newfound pessimism about the human condition. It is, after all, an almost unthinking optimism about the present and the future that makes teaching and learning consequential, and I still honor that perception, particularly where the young are concerned. Having devoted most of my life to the search for and dissemination of knowledge, I needed to affirm that it had been worthwhile. I was therefore implacably resolved, even if it turned out to be for no one's benefit but my own, to create something that emphasized the sanguine rather than the bloody. (A modest enough resolution, I thought). To accomplish this, I sought to focus my thoughts on some truly auspicious element, some lustrous vein of gold, shining forth from what was to me an otherwise dismal human landscape.

There are several such rare and precious human gifts to admire and celebrate. I might have concentrated on music, or artistic expression, or spirituality, or altruism, or some similar high human talents that are all in equally short supply—if I were other than who I am. Being no Schoenberg, Kandinsky, Thoreau, or Condorcet, these happy blessings were not for me to explore in depth. (Nor could I dwell on more common human glories, such as sex or humor. Being neither a du Barry nor a Dave Barry, I ruled these out also.) My nature and experience directed me, instead, to celebrate that marvelous and uniquely human virtue, rationality, and to sing the praises of its most significant offspring, modern Western science. This is not to say that I think rationality is the be-all and end-all of human existence, but rather that I see it as a vital and exhilarating part of life, a part that is too little appreciated in the society at large. By writing this book, I have elected to engage with other rationalists and potential rationalists, who live in, and have to cope with, a decidedly irrational world. I believe that those who appreciate rationality as a way of life should revel in their unusual capacity to do so. They should come out of the closet. Even as the world around them disparages it, they should constantly ply their powers of reason and absorb into their daily lives the deep knowledge that has been, and will continue to be, attained by the exercise of rationality. But they must enjoy the splendid feast of reason humanely and with sensitivity, without isolating themselves from, or dismissing the needs of, the world around them. Whatever their many differences, human beings are One only; we all carry the same stigmata.

The main purpose of this book is to encourage rationalists to achieve concurrently these ends of self-fulfillment and service to life. As such, the book is not meant to be a prescription for curing all the ills of the world, for which purpose I have neither ambition nor confident reassurance to offer. For reasons that will be made clear in what follows, I do not entertain high hopes that rationality or scientific knowledge alone can overturn the self-deluding and self-destructive ways of a world that is fundamentally indifferent or even hostile to them.

Because this book focuses on rationality, it is of necessity unsympathetic to irrational beliefs that are widely and deeply held in modern Western societies. But it is not my object to offend people who share such beliefs, although I suspect that is unavoidable. Much less am I concerned to try to convert them to rationality. I am under no quixotic illusion, as many rationalists from the Enlightenment on have been; I do not think that it is only a matter of time before the fog of fantasy will be completely lifted before the blaze of reason. On the contrary, I believe that irrationality is a surpassing fact of life. It is an ineradicable and overriding compulsion of most human beings, one of many fateful genetic residues from our evolutionary past. Shakespeare said it about his era, but really for all time: we must cope with "the temper of the times / when madmen lead the blind." All the more reason that the power of rationality be continually honored and rejoiced in, so as to maintain and extend its arduous and precarious grip on human affairs.

In considering this book, the reader may also find it helpful to know something about my political and social beliefs, as I suspect that some, affronted by one or another of my opinions or assertions, will seriously question those beliefs. On the political side, I remain what I was in my youth, a left-of-center New Deal Democrat, which I suppose makes me a flaming liberal on the present-day American political scene. By "liberal" I understand someone who truly believes in, rather than just prates about, the birthrights of each individual human being and who upholds the view that the principal purpose of society is "the greatest good for the greatest number." This does not require accepting irrational beliefs to be as worthy as scientifically founded ones, just because the majority may favor them. It is not necessarily illiberal to think that the majority is often poorly informed and therefore likely to be wrong. Furthermore, it will become clear in what follows that I am confident in the reliability of other unorthodoxies: that none of our traditional religions or their deities warrant our credence; that our genes play a major role in determining our behaviors, including intelligence; that free market capitalism is not the consummate achievement of human culture; and that poverty in America is not necessarily a self-inflicted crime. I am therefore in most respects an unreconstructed and possibly dangerous heretic: I am a resolute rationalist, a political liberal, a confirmed atheist, a genetic partisan, and an economic proletarian. Read on at your own peril.

This book is directed to the general reader who is interested in the powers of rationality. Some of the ideas are scientific ones, but they are presented so that one does not have to be a scientist to understand them. Nevertheless, the book does not lend itself to speed reading. It is meant to be accessible to the intelligent nonscientist, but at the same time challenging. I hope the experience is like eating a fine whole lobster—part of it is easy, but some of it takes determination. I am continually amazed by the way that quite intelligent people sometimes misread and flagrantly misrepresent a written text. There is apparently a mental quirk that occasionally operates to transmute what is there in black and white into what a reader wants to believe is written. The more unorthodox and disturbing a book is, it seems, the more likely that misreading may occur. I can only echo Ben Jonson in this: "Pray thee, take care, that tak'st my book in hand. / To read it well: that is to understand."

I want to be very clear that this book is not intended as a work of original or rigorous scholarship. I have read a fair amount of relevant material, but I have certainly not read exhaustively on the many subjects in the book. Consequently, there well may be some serious omissions or unlearned neglect in the work; if so, this is inadvertent. In general, I have preferred to think things out for myself. I often took great pleasure in finding that someone had already thought and written much the same thing, and I was then happy to affirm that he or she had done so earlier than I. Nor is this book a work of scientific exactitude in all aspects. Terms such as *rationality*, like *intelligence* (or *beauty*, for that matter), cannot even be defined precisely and scientifically or to everyone's satisfaction. As a scientist addicted to scientific precision, I well realize that I am venturing into, for me, uncharted waters. Hence I present this book not so much to establish eternal truths where controversy now exists, but rather as a personal commentary, one man's thoughtful memoir, rehearsing the strange paradox of the high glories and the low estate of rationality in modern society.

A few words about this book's contents and organization. The first chapter considers the nature of rationality and analyzes who our modern-day rationalists are. I go on to consider the dual worlds that they and everyone else confront: their own internal world and the external world we all share. While recognizing that it is the internal world that is primary for each human being, I aim to illuminate the nature of the external world. In Chapter 2, I explore primitive people's prescientific views of the external world. Of particular interest is how they came to devise the myths and religions that brought their formidable and hostile world into an anthropocentric focus, in order to serve imperative human needs and to help people survive—and how in the process Man created God. For a rationalist, this mythical scheme of the external world is no longer tenable. In Chapter 3, I begin a journey into the world of modern science. I describe how scientific analysis was transformed about 400 years ago and led to a powerful method of establishing scientific truth and an understanding of the reality of the external world. The new method was first successfully applied to cosmology, the physics of the Heavens. Then, in Chapter 4, we enter the realm of biology, the science of life, humanity's oldest subject and, in many respects, its newest analytical science. It is also humanity's most deeply relevant, and most complex, natural science.

In the succession of Chapters 4 through 9, I survey the central ideas of modern biology for the intelligent lay reader. I deal with the scientific knowledge recently acquired about the panorama of molecular and cellular mechanisms that carry out life's chemical processes of energy production, of growth and development, of reproduction, and of evolution. These mechanisms illuminate the nature of and limits on human life, survival, and death; for a rationalist, they obliterate the myths and fantasies about them that still occupy the irrational world. It is becoming clear that our genes exercise a strong influence on our behavior, although the detailed dissection of this influence remains to be achieved. I also explore what we have learned about how evolution has functioned for billions of years to sustain life on this planet and how our widespread ignorance of these evolutionary survival mechanisms is having catastrophic consequences.

How a rationalist can achieve the difficult but essential synergy of the dual worlds of human beings, the vastly different egocentric internal and the scientific external worlds, is the vital subject of Chapter 10; here I develop Nils Bohr's idea of complementarity to cope with this duality. Finally, the last chapter delves into the enigma of the real world and its irrational and necessarily chaotic operations. I examine how a rationalist can not only survive but, one hopes, thrive in it.

After completing the book, I realize that this is a tremendous range of subject matter to be covered adequately in such a small volume. In thinking about the book's brevity, I suspect that it is in good part a result of my life-long conformity to the kind of succinctness required for writing professional scientific research papers. Scientists become trained to say something only once, and without entertaining embellishment. This sometimes makes for rather a staccato style. It puts scientists at a disadvantage with respect to their colleagues in the humanities, who seem to agree that only by paraphrasing each thought five or six times, preferably consecutively, can an argument be made sufficiently compelling. This is my first book. It is possible that in my books to come I will do better, repeat things five or six times, add some anecdotal trivia, and fill more pages.

A few words of acknowledgment and gratitude are in order. That I would finally write this book was by no means a foregone conclusion several years ago. In fact, it would never have gone beyond the stage of some collected thoughts most likely left unpublished if it were not for the constant encouragement, as well as superlative comments and suggestions, of several friends; so I hope that you will blame them if you don't care for the book. These worthies include Professors Russell F. Doolittle, Melford Spiro, and Avrum Stroll, all colleagues at the University of California at San Diego, and Edward O. Wilson of Harvard University. They have helped to see me and this book through a difficult time. I am also grateful to Dr. Anne H. Dutton for her help on research matters. Mrs. Myrtali Anagnostopoulos has graced the book with her drawings of Figure 1 and Figures A through E. And above all I want to thank my wife, Ruth Elizabeth Singer, because, being an eternal optimist, she has suffered through my abiding pessimism and has managed to do so unyieldingly but loyally.

CHAPTER I

Homage to the Square

This book is a celebration of rationality and rationalists. And they are eminently worthy of celebration. It is the human mind, with its capacity for reason, that is the special mark that evolution has set upon humanity. It is what distinguishes us as a unique presence in the world, perhaps in the entire universe. After all, in what other respect than the mind and its extraordinary force of reason are human beings so special? We cannot fly like a bird, we cannot subsist without water like a camel, we cannot race like a cheetah, we cannot use the sun's energy like a plant, and we do not smell like a rose. Absent the brain (as unfortunately too often appears to be the case), the human is a very ordinary creature. Furthermore, as a factual measure of the great value the human animal invests in its brain, a newborn's brain consumes 60 percent of all the energy a baby takes in. (That figure would be more like

5 percent if it were simply proportional to the relative weight of the newborn's brain.) Rationality, therefore, is one of the crowning distinctions of humanity.

Strangely enough, though, reason can hardly be said to illuminate human affairs. Instead, reason seems often to be only a candle flickering in the darkness created by human greed, aggression, and ignorance. The history of humanity, the saga of the several million years' existence of the genus *Homo*, is a story of the only gradual and limited intrusion of rationality into the complex burden of the human experience. This encroachment of reason into a quite irrational world has been painfully slow, imperfect, and often unwelcome. Nevertheless, it is reason that has revolutionized human existence. The elaborate technological structure of modern Western society, which has brought us out of a forested jungle into a cement and steel one, has largely resulted from the application of rational methods to human physical activities. Likewise, all the scientific understanding of the universe and of the nature of life that has been magnificently constructed in only the past few hundred years has been achieved by an uncommon group of people of rational temper. This understanding has completely transformed thinking people's views of the world around them. It was also rationalist thinkers of the Enlightenment, such as John Locke, Tom Paine, and Thomas Jefferson, who championed the principles of popular governance and the rights of man, ideas that, revolutionary at the time, have since remade Western political life. Although the influence of rationality on the human condition has been limited, it has clearly had substantial consequences. Even so, rationalists, having so extensively shaped the character of our society, have never had much impact on how it has functioned.

Creative intelligence has transformed the world but has rarely ruled it.
Now that we have glimpsed some of the extraordinary ac-
complishments of rationality and rationalists, what do these terms
mean? Who are the rationalists among us, and what is it that characterizes them? *Rationality*, like many other terms in wide usage,
is a concept that we think we know but, when pressed, have difficulty in precisely defining. I venture this concise definition: rationality is the use of intelligence and reason to seek the truth ob-
jectively and without prejudice. I recognize that this version is
loaded with words that themselves require definition; for our general purposes, though, this definition will do.

More difficult is the definition of a rationalist. This is because
every human being functions both rationally and irrationally. In
this book, it is rationality that is accorded special prominence.
However, irrationality is not to be discounted: it is an inborn and
powerful human predilection. Irrationality can be defined as any
mental activity that largely escapes or denies our rational control.
Our subconscious selves, our emotions, passions, turbulences,
perversities—all contribute intensely to our irrational side. Some
forms that irrationality takes are benign and are even among the
most noble of human attributes—the love of beauty and much of
the creation and enjoyment of art and poetry derive richly from
the emotions and the subconscious. (As John Keats once wrote
to a friend, "O for a life of Sensations rather than a life of
Thoughts!") Further, irrationality is often the prime source of the
hope that springs eternal even in a rationalist's breast. Rationality can sometimes put hope in jeopardy: "Hope is only man's mis-
trust of the clear foresight of his mind," wrote that great human-
ist and rationalist Paul Valéry. But without hope, life can be a
depressing wasteland. Besides its brighter aspects, however, irra-

tionality has its darker side. It is the source of much of the superstition, absurdity, and violence that permeate our world. So it is clearly a mixed blessing.

While everyone is a complex mixture of rational and irrational elements, each person exhibits a different effective balance among these elements. I propose to define as rationalists those who demonstrate a much higher than average proportion of rationality over irrationality in the conduct of their lives. For rationalists of contemporary times, such conduct involves seven unusual features.

First, these individuals consciously elect to have reason and rationality be the guiding lights of their lives; and they have the capacity and courage to confront all aspects of reality with a minimum of illusions, compromises, and subjectivity.

Second, they prize knowledge and have a high esteem for scientific knowledge. Rationalists need to have some basic scientific literacy and empathy, but by no means are their ranks restricted to professional scientists. Conversely, a significant proportion of scientists may not necessarily be rationalists, if the rationality they employ in pursuit of their professional interests is narrow and doesn't carry over to other aspects of their lives, for example, to religious matters.

Third, rationalists are prepared to seek the truth wherever it takes them, which may often pit their views against the conventional wisdom of the majority. They are therefore not distressed if they choose to adhere to a minority point of view; indeed, they expect to have to do so often.

Fourth, they do not compartmentalize their rationality but rather attempt to extend it into any and all appropriate aspects of their lives.

Fifth, although I recognize the likelihood of arousing controversy over this, I nevertheless firmly believe that modern ratio-

nalists, informed by the knowledge gained by biological evolution and anthropology, no longer can accept the dogmas of any
of the traditional religions, including belief in the existence of
their gods. To rationalists, traditional religions have become the
quintessential celebration of the irrational.

Sixth, rationalists are sworn enemies of hypocrisy, the first and
last refuge of many irrationalists. As a consequence, a rationalist
in our society is like the uncorrupted child who, almost alone
among the multitude of those who see that the Emperor is stark
naked, cannot pretend otherwise.

And, seventh, they have open minds. Rationalists are pragma-
tists, not unthinking believers. They recognize a major lesson of
history; namely, that all institutions—religious, political, and economic—are mortal. Institutions are born and mature in times that
are favorable for their success; but as times and conditions change,
they eventually decay. Often, institutions may already be in an advanced stage of senescence just when appearances most loudly
proclaim their triumph. Rationalists are always ready to subject
all ideas and institutions to scrutiny, however sacrosanct they may
be deemed by the majority in society.

These characteristics of and criteria for rationalists are not absolute or valid for all times and circumstances. They are not en-
graved on any tablets. Many readers might prefer to delete some
criteria or add others. What emerges from this or any comparable set of criteria, however, is the clear inference that rationalists
represent only a small fraction of the human population. The balance between rationality and irrationality in any individual is, as
with most human behaviors, quite likely to be genetically determined (Chapter 6); and those who are more highly rational are
genetically less frequent. I estimate that today's rationalists, as I

have defined them, account for less than 10 percent of the population. A Gallup poll taken in the 1980s indicated that only about 9 percent of the American people did not believe that God created man.[1] Some 50 percent believed that God created man within the past 10,000 years; another 41 percent believed that God created man more than 10,000 years ago—all of this gullibility 150 years after the emergence of the theory of evolution. Referring to the fifth criterion, I would consider no more than the 9 percent as true rationalists. In a different context, other polls have tried to assess the scientific literacy of the American public. One such poll sponsored by the National Science Foundation arrived at the estimate that only about 8 percent of Americans had even minimal scientific literacy[2]—our second criterion for a rationalist. These numbers therefore accord with my guess that rationalists constitute a maximum of about 10 percent of our society. The exact number, in any event, is not the most important consideration. What is significant is the conclusion that rationalists make up only a small minority of the citizenry. Besides, since rationalists are more aware of overpopulation problems than are irrationalists, they may elect to have fewer offspring and hence may be fated to become an ever-shrinking fraction of society's members.

Rationality is related to, but is not the same as, intelligence. Many intelligent people do not fit the definition of a rationalist by virtue of not meeting at least some of the criteria indicated. Many people value the emotional and irrational aspects of life much more than they value rationality. Much great art, literature, and music, reflecting the feelings aroused by the colors, shapes, and inner voices of the world, are among the creations of irrational high intelligence. Rationalists are therefore a subset of intelligent people. What is more, rationality is not related to altruism. Altruism that is directed beyond one's immediate family and clan is an independent human behavior that unfortunately is also in short supply. So people who are both rational and altruistic are probably altogether only a precious few. Put another way, it is unhappily likely that many more heartless rationalists are around than altruistic ones. In public life, however, a brain without a heart "draws nectar in a sieve." But I will not address this issue in this book. Perhaps someone else more suited to it than I will write "The Splendid Feast of Altruism," without simply reducing it to inclusive fitness or an exercise in game theory.

That rationalists constitute only a small minority of the population is reflected in many ways. For one, the aspiration for knowledge that motivates rationalists has often been viewed with morbid suspicion by the society at large. The bloody fury of the gods unleashed on Prometheus for revealing the knowledge of fire to humanity exemplifies how human beings have often pictured their gods as jealously guarding knowledge from them. Likewise, Adam and Eve forever debased man and woman by eating the fruit of the Tree of Knowledge and thereby ingesting a comprehension of Good and Evil—a capability that God apparently did not want His favorite creation to have. In his later years, the Preacher avowed that "he who increaseth knowledge increaseth sorrow," a sentiment calculated to freeze the blood of any rationalist. Dr. Faustus's soul became forever Satan's property when he sought knowledge considered by medieval society to be beyond what a human being ought properly to possess. To elevate scientific knowledge above Biblical truth was a certain way to court death during the Counter-Reformation, as Galileo, a devout Catholic of his time but a supreme rationalist in all other respects, discovered. In our time, things haven't changed all that much: ridicule is often heaped on the "square," the "nerd," and the "egghead." Even Einstein, with his unruly crown of hair and his baggy pants, was revered by the public not so much for his rational genius but more as someone touched by God, in the same way that the Russian masses once held their village idiots in holy awe. While society has usually eagerly accepted the practical gifts of the applications of rationality, it has generally had an uneasy and unappreciative relation with the rationalists themselves. Society, when it hasn't ridiculed rationalists, has often pitied them as misfits, much as, in the fable, the sparrow pitied the peacock the burden of his tail.

Many of the directions being energetically pursued in Westernized cultures, largely supported by the majority of irrationalists in the society, are often anathema to concerned rationalists. Simply put, the lowest common denominator prevails in modern culture, politics, and morality. Many rationalists have therefore become aliens in a society that their kind did so much to create. Adult rationalists, particularly women, are brought to question whether their rationality isn't a disadvantage in today's society. Men don't like lasses whose intellect surpasses. Equally dreadful is the need of the young to hide the light of their budding rationality under a bushel in order to gain acceptance among their irrational peers.

Because I wanted to help myself, and, I hope, others of rationalist bent—especially those entering the adult world—to surmount these circumstances, I decided to write this book. It is intended to be a guide for myself and other rationalists to learn to rejoice in the wonderful gift of rationality and to consider how best to incorporate it into our lives. In celebrating reason, I dwell on its magnificent offspring, science. The profound understanding about the nature of humanity and of the universe that has been the flowering of science must be embraced by thinking persons into a meaningful philosophy of living.

· · ·

How will rationalists make sense of their lives, especially in view of the irrationality that reigns around them? *That* is the question. Not whether to be, or not to be. Each of us gets a free admission to this Globe; it would be churlish to walk out before the performance ends. And once we have left, we will never be allowed in again. So it is best to learn to bear with the whips and scorns of time (not to mention the slings and arrows, the contumely, the fardels, and more, of an often malign world), to brace and fortify oneself in order to enjoy life to the fullest and to savor the splendid feast of reason.

For each of us, the beginning and the end of everything is the self, which is our internal world. This internal world is the rich treasure house of thought, sensations, emotions, and passions; as such, it is also the primary domain of human irrationality. The internal world centers on our mental being, both conscious and unconscious, and the actions taken in response to the dictates of the mind. It is the world of Descartes's first principle of existence: "I think, therefore I am." The internal world is by its nature completely egocentric. It has always been, and always will be, the one unimpeachable reality of an individual's existence. It therefore forms the crucial center of every human life. But each of us also perceives an external world around us, one that is primarily material rather than mental. This material world, which includes one's own body, consists of one's surroundings, the multitude of objects in the sky, the powerful forces of nature, and the great diversity of other inhabitants of the earth, all of which each of us becomes aware of and must contend with as we mature. What is one to make of this external world? How does our self, isolated and sovereign, relate to it? This book is essentially devoted to these questions. While I affirm that the internal world of human beings is the vital core of our existence, that is not the world that I explore in depth here. I concentrate instead on our external world, while acknowledging freely that the internal world is, and must be, primary to each person.

The conscious awareness of an external world is a uniquely human attribute, a hallmark of our rationality. Only very recently in history have humans begun to achieve an objective scientific understanding of the external world. By contrast, for almost all of humanity's several million years of existence, our views of the external world were completely subjective; they were *solely* a reflection of our internal world. As we have become more confident of our powers, our benighted and aboriginal views of the external world have become more and more centered on ourselves; that is, we constructed an *anthropocentric* externality.

These views originated from needs to propitiate the vast forces of nature that could destroy us, to console us for our inevitable death, and to magnify our sense of significance in a complex and bewildering world that altogether dwarfed us. A myriad of primitive views of the nature of human beings and their external world were therefore elaborated in different societies over time. Many of these views were remarkable for their ingenuity and beauty, but they were all anthropocentric offshoots of an egocentric internal world. Many often sought to dignify these inventions by attributing to them a divine origin or inspiration. Even so, these views have never evinced any autonomous and objective reality. Nevertheless, over the millennia most people came to accept one or another of them unquestioningly.

The most extraordinary of the many remarkable consequences of the rise and maturation of modern science, starting only about 400 years ago, has been to provide a singular, spectacular, and verifiably objective view of the external world. The scientific view, though derived by human minds in the context of the society of which we are a part, for the *first time* transcends our egocentric internal world and is essentially independent of it. Like mathematics, the scientific view of the external world has by now attained its own autonomy from the evanescent human condition. Even though this scientific view is incomplete—and continues to be adjusted and expanded by scientific investigation—its outlines and many of its details are already secure. Many features of the rational scientific picture of the external world are conceptually quite revolutionary, often completely at odds with many traditional anthropocentric views. The facts ascertained by science show that many of these traditional views are fictions. Partly because they are relatively recent, though, these scientific ideas have so far had little effect on majority views of the external world. By and large, the old anthropocentric views, even if somewhat shaken, still prevail in a society that is fundamentally irrational.

Majority opinions, however, are irrelevant to scientific truth. We have never held a plebiscite to determine whether 2 plus 2 equals 4, or whether the Earth is round or flat. Rationalists understand that science has provided an awesome, astonishing, and ever-deepening insight to the reality of the external world, an insight that is not subject to opinion uninformed by facts. Science is the sturdy saxifrage that has split the rock of dense delusion.

As the book proceeds, I examine and contrast the anthropocentric and scientific views of the external world. Most of this is not new ground, but it needs to be continually reasserted above the noise and clamor of our irrational world. My ultimate object is to suggest a rational conciliation of the internal egocentric world of an individual human being with the vastly different cosmic world that envelopes us; this juncture occurs in Chapter 10.

CHAPTER 2

Making the External World Safe for Humanity
The Roles of Myth and Religion

Terror of the unknown must have been a constant burden of primitive man and woman. They would have found the external world dangerous and hostile, and unpredictably so. They must have stood in awe and fear of the overwhelming forces of nature, unleashed with little warning and with no apparent design. Lashing rainstorms and floods, deafening thunder and eerie lightning, raging fires, calamitous earthquakes and volcanic upheavals from the bowels of the earth, turbulent seas, and terrible droughts, all brought puny humans to a frightening awareness of their powerlessness and fragility in an uncontrollable world. Powerful animals threatened their lives; other animals eluded their capture. Would they eat or be eaten? They dreaded the death that struck so often and feared the power and malice of the dead.

But an indomitable will to survive, together with their ever-developing brains, led human beings to construct imaginary worlds to help them cope with this perilous environment. In the absence of any scientific understanding, the universal response of primitive people to their predicament was to mythologize this alien and material world, to animate it with mythical living and immortal beings who were more powerful than humans and who could control the awesome forces of nature, beings with whom humans could identify and to whom they could turn in supplication in times of need. We rationalists must admiringly acknowledge that, for their time, these mythologies constituted a remarkably sophisticated achievement, ranking in brilliance with any ever created in history. The invention and elaboration of mythologies of a natural world inhabited by superhumans and eventually human-like deities generated a more pliant and friendlier kind of external world to in which to live. What had previously been an utterly forbidding and unapproachable external world became humanized, a mythical outgrowth of human life, which rendered that external world no longer foreign and autonomous but instead anthropocentric, focused on humans. All of this extraordinary achievement must have required a prolonged period of pre-recorded history to construct, and it eventually took on an immense variety of highly imaginative forms in different primitive societies.

A great Babel of myths ultimately arose, investing variously the heavenly bodies, the forces of nature, different kinds of animals, the mountains, and the oceans with superhuman character and functions. These myths were handed down from generation to generation, and some were eventually recorded. Beyond their utility in confronting a hostile world, myths and other fabulous inventions gave free rein to the creativity of the human imagination—the planting of a world of dreams into the soil of reality. As expressions of that creativity, myths often show delightful imagery and great poetic beauty.

Mythic notions, and the practices of occult magic and worship that derived from them, eventually were refined and permuted into more formal religions. Mythology probably first arose in hunter-gatherer societies, well before the invention of the technology of agriculture only about 10,000 years ago. The introduction of agriculture, however, completely transformed the human societies that practiced it. By providing, for the first time in human history, both a stable source of food and a means of generating wealth, agriculture helped to change humanity's view of itself: rather than seeing themselves as just another group of powerless and completely subservient creatures in the world, human beings began to perceive themselves as sentient beings that were unique among, and superior to, all the other animals around them. With the rapid growth of great city-states and the beginnings of sophisticated urban life that were made possible by the advent of agriculture, humanity's view of the external world as anthropocentric was greatly enhanced, as echoed in the following paean to Man:

> For us the winds do blow,
> The earth doth rest, heaven move, and fountains flow.
> Nothing we see but means our good,
> As our delight or as our treasure;
> The whole is either our cupboard of food,
> Or cabinet of pleasure.
>
> *— George Herbert, 1633*

The proud human race now occupied the center, and became the very purpose, of God's Creation of the Universe.[1] The Earth was the focal body of that Universe and was given over to human beings to subdue. Thus, primitive myths were gradually superseded by more sophisticated anthropocentric religions, administered by powerful priesthoods who formalized and codified beliefs into doctrines and faiths.

Although all religions share core objectives because they all serve in different ways the same needs of humankind, their diversity over time is staggering. Most believers are convinced that they are in possession of the one true faith. A. F. C. Wallace, however, estimates that 100,000 religions have existed over the course of human history.[2] Every social group has had its own religion and its own deities, isolated initially by the limited range of experience of the world's peoples and minimal communication with other groups. Think of it: a hundred thousand doctrines, each unique and unchallengeable because of its divine origin. Which is more equal than all the others? Even into the present, the world's religions remain diverse—some pantheistic, some polytheistic, some trinitarian, and some monotheistic.

One significant function of myths and religions is that they provide to the curious a prescientific story about how the external world first arose. Most of them prescribe a unique cosmogony, which is usually parochial because the people who invented it were parochial. Island societies, for example, like those of Japan and Micronesia, mythologized a Genesis in which the crucial event was the divine creation of their own native islands, raised up within the primeval, unfurrowed ocean. Many thousands of myths and religions have each invoked a special divine creation of the first man and woman, from whom its devotees were, of course, the chosen among all human descendants. Some myths and religions have elaborated afterlives for their believers after death. Afterlives satisfy our tenacious fantasy of personal immortality, as well as prod us into worshipful good behavior here on Earth, thus ensuring that we wind up in Heaven instead of Hell for all eternity.

Rationalists nowadays have no use for the claims made by any of the traditional religions to a divine origin and a uniquely revealed truth. Such religions appear to rationalists to have been transparently concocted by their ancestors in order to cope with the world. The individual claims to uniqueness made by various religions are simply irreconcilable with the long evolution of religious thought and practices in isolated human societies and with the enormous diversity of religions, dogmas, and deities over historical time. Rather, these facts argue that all religions have been the inventions of different groups of people and that none is the result of divine revelation or inspiration. Who is to say that one or another religion is divinely revealed but that all others are not? Usually the gods betray their human creation: how wonderful that they look just like their chosen people, as in Michelangelo's ceiling in the Sistine Chapel. It has also been very useful that each god, besides looking like the chosen group of people—be they Aztec, Dyak, Hebrew, or Zulu—also happens to speak their language.

To a confirmed rationalist having some understanding of science, anthropocentric views of the external world, as fostered by traditional religions and their dogmas, have no credibility whatsoever. They are based on nothing but prescientific fantasies and inventions about the nature of the world, designed to help humans to survive in it. The Hebrew Bible is a work of great wisdom, but it was written by humans about the human condition;

it does not—it could not—reflect the true origins or nature of material existence. The universe, and life on Earth, turns out to be immensely more complex and intricate than any prescientific minds could possibly have imagined.

Having arrived at this conclusion, a rationalist must nevertheless acknowledge the ubiquity and extraordinary power of traditional religious beliefs in the modern world. The reasons for this are clear. For one, most individuals in our society are, from childhood on, continuously conditioned to accept religious belief. This early and intense indoctrination is very difficult to overcome, even for people of rational temper. Furthermore, many of us are broken by personal tragedies and are desperate for the kind of consolation religion can provide. Religions still serve the critical needs of the many for whom rationality offers neither comprehension nor satisfaction. For those who are capable of only limited rational analysis, established religions provide many of life's essentials: a deeply moving and exalted story of the meaning and purpose of all existence; a haven of peace in a contentious world that they do not understand and cannot control; consolation for unjustified misfortunes and unhappy fates; a means of transcending death, the inescapable end of earthly experience; the imposition of a sense of purposeful order on an otherwise chaotic existence, by means of set rituals and prescribed practices; a cohesive social focus for individuals, in groups of those who share a set of religious beliefs; an ethical foundation for society, based on the certainty of ineffable, eternal rewards for good behavior; a means of coping with the mysteries of the world and the overwhelming forces of nature; the promise of eternal life to the blessed; a source of spiritual inspiration for artistic expression; and a means for even the lowliest to enjoy a spiritual passion beyond self and to experience an exaltation by communion with some Greater Being. The persistence—indeed, the flourishing—of traditional and especially fundamentalist religions in an Age of Science is therefore no mystery. For the irrationalist majority in modern Western society, unassailed by rationalist doubts, religions supply indispensable benefits and will continue to do so for the foreseeable future. To believe otherwise is a delusion.

To a thinking person in today's world, however, as attractive as these benefits of traditional religions are, the cost of abandoning rationality in order to embrace them is much too great. It would involve a betrayal of the innermost self and the adoption of a level of hypocrisy that is altogether unacceptable. A rationalist has to find ways other than through traditional religions to fulfill some of the same intense human needs that religions satisfy for their faithful. The anthropocentric view of the external world does not accord with reality. For a thinking person, therefore, the scientific knowledge of the real world needs to be made a cornerstone of his or her life. As I contend further on (Chapter 10), this knowledge of the nature of the external world can provide a rationalist with some of the same benefits that religion supplies to the irrationalist.

I have so far refrained from castigating traditional religions for the sometimes barbarous behavior that religious fervor has engendered in believers without any restraint—indeed, often with encouragement—from their religious leaders. Furthermore, once traditional religions and their dogmas have become established, they have often stood against freedom of inquiry, staging book burnings, proclaiming fatwahs, and the like; and their priesthoods have often served as staunch supporters of the rich and the powerful. These deplorable aspects of traditional religions should not be overlooked, but they are not the primary basis of my opposition to them. That opposition is instead founded on the irrationality of religious beliefs and dogmas as I have described them.

I turn now to the view of the external world derived by modern science. First I review briefly the remarkable origins of that science, dating back only about 400 years ago in the West. I elaborate on its claims to truth as contrasted with those of protoscientific pursuits of earlier times. Then I examine the understanding of the universe and of the nature of life that has been the glorious golden fruit of the Tree of Scientific Knowledge.

CHAPTER 3

Deciphering the Real World

Primitive people, at least those of a more rational bent, must have been amazed by, and intensely curious about, the world they inhabited. The most common of natural phenomena were—and still are—a source of wonder and awe: the ever-recurring cycles of night and day and the seasons; the blazing sun and its companion, the serene but ever-changing moon; the intricate patterns of stars, along with the special few wanderers, the planets, moving among them each with its own special trajectory; and then life, with the miracle of birth and the mystery of death; the enormous variety of marvelously different creatures abounding; the gorgeous colors and wonderful aromas of this Eden. What was the nature of these ever-astonishing phenomena? How did they first arise? Protoscientific observations of these everyday wonders must have occurred in all prehistoric cultures and then blossomed in societies that arose after the Agricultural Revolution, when some thinking people were liberated from the daily regimen of survival to indulge their ability to reason.

In most early societies, such protoscience was anthropocentric, as was religion, and narrowly reflected the needs and interests of society and its rulers. Thus the earliest detailed observations of the stars and planets (astronomy) were often directed to the divination of future events (such as eclipses) and to the avoidance of catastrophes supposedly associated with them. Protoscience was closely allied to the practice of magic in these cultures. In more advanced societies, protoscientific views became more sophisticated, but they were often permeated with the idea of purpose or design. The human race and the universe did not simply *exist*. Rather, there had to be a purpose to their creation and existence; and these early attempts to understand the detailed nature of the world started from, and were irrevocably tied to, such purpose. The extraordinary protoscience of the Greeks, from about 600 B.C. on, the most advanced of the ancient world, was imbued with this sense of purpose and design. It dictated a duality of the world: the Earth and the Heavens were purposefully of an entirely different nature. All change, all things crass and imperfect were confined to the lowly Earth, the abode of humanity. The remote and silent Heavens (the moon and beyond), however, were perfect and unchanging, the abode of the gods. Even the composition of the Earth and that of the Heavens were considered to be different. The former consisted of the four elements—fire, air, earth, and water—in a state of continual flux; the latter contained a special and permanent heavenly fifth element (from which we derive the word *quintessence*). Perfection of the Heavens meant to the Greeks, with their comparatively highly developed geometry and physics, that all heavenly objects had to be smooth-surfaced and spherical in form and that their motion was perfect, namely, circular and unvarying in velocity.

The imposition of the notion of either special meaning or purpose on protoscientific thinking has invariably been completely stultifying to attempts to understand the reality of the world. Whether secular or religious, such preconceptions have dictated paralyzing constraints on the acquisition of true scientific knowledge. The universe turns out to be much too complicated—indeed, thrillingly so—and humans too minor a physical presence in it—indeed, depressingly so—to be understood by embracing one simplistic and anthropocentric overview as the starting point.

It is difficult for us today to comprehend how little was known about the external world just a few hundred years ago. The rationalists of an earlier time were clever and numerous enough, but they were at an utter impasse. They did not even have any sound notion of what aspects of the world it might be feasible to understand (perhaps only very few?) or how to proceed to find out about them. Rationalists of that era were generally religious believers, partly because Christianity was so all-persuasive in the West, but mostly because there was as yet no adequate alternative: the scientific account of the external world did not exist. To understand that world, there first had to be introduced a radically different and systematic approach to its study. This new method, quite remarkable in its austerity and modesty, was eventually engendered in the seventeenth century, mainly by Galileo Galilei and several other independent thinkers, notably René Descartes. The following simple but revolutionary proposals were advanced.

To make real progress in understanding the world, we must take a wholly different and systematic approach, as compared with past efforts. We must make a new start, beginning with the basics and working up to greater complexity—not, as previously, starting from the top (imposing a grand design) and working down. All values that are extraneous to the material world, such as religious doctrine or anthropocentrism, are to be set aside.

The nature of the world is to be investigated with the tools of mathematics so as to subject knowledge to mathematical rigor and precision. Therefore, one should concentrate *for scientific purposes only* on properties in the world that can be assigned quantity (numbers). Time, mass, length, area, volume, and velocity are items that can be usefully studied; emotions, feelings, ethical values, and other nonquantifiable properties cannot. It is important to appreciate that this does not constitute a value judgment about these properties: the velocity of an object is not regarded by scientists as more important than its beauty. It is instead a strictly utilitarian exercise. The exclusion of nonquantifiable properties from the scientific study of existence might seem to be severely limiting, but what is left can be treated with, and be required to conform to, mathematical logic and rigor.

In protoscientific (for example, Greek) times, reason and common sense were generally used to figure out the relationships among several properties (variables), such as the relationship between the mass, the velocity, and the time it took an object in free fall. What was deemed reasonable was often accepted as true, without requiring any but the most perfunctory experimental verification. In the new procedure, however, accurate experiments constituted an essential line of attack in order to establish such relationships quantitatively. Experiments based on numerical analysis were to be designed and carried out to determine the precise change in one variable that accompanied a change in another, with all other variables kept unchanged. General laws governing such relationships might be derived and tested against such experimental data. This experimental procedure, of isolating entities or variables from their natural surroundings and studying them in a controlled environment in which all other variables are kept constant, is at the heart of reductionism; it is reductionism that has been the cornerstone of all modern science. (In Chapter 8, I explore the close connection between reductionist practice and the concept of fixed functionality.) Galileo's experiments leading to the discovery of the first law of motion are examples of reductionist science. They are as admirable 400 years later as they were ingenious and remarkable at the time.[1]

This combined experimental and mathematical approach to the study of the natural world was responsible for the birth of modern science. It is such a commonplace today that we are often startled to realize that this *modus operandi* was only so recently introduced. This was not, however, the only enduring legacy of the work of Galileo. Equally important were the definition of scientific truth as that established by the new approach and the insistence on the primacy of that scientific truth over authority-dictated truth, whether of secular or religious origin. Until the sixteenth century in the West, the two primary sources of truth were Aristotle and the Bible, the latter considered unassailable as the word of God. Thus, when Copernicus's heliocentric model of the solar system was finally published in 1543, only after his death, the Church treated it as a clever and harmless mathematical exercise, no more, even though it seemed to contravene Scripture. Martin Luther's reaction to Copernicus's work was to scoff at it: "Doesn't the fool know that Joshua bade the sun [not the Earth] to stand still?" Nowadays we may laugh at Luther's remark as naïve, forgetting that at the time it was an entirely warranted expression of the inviolability of Biblical truth and the insignificance of any other claim to truth. But when Galileo, less than a century later, became convinced by his telescopic observations that Copernicus's heliocentric model was a better description of the solar system than the 2,000-year-old geocentric model of Aristotle and Ptolemy, he challenged the primacy of authority-dictated truth and, in particular, Biblical truth regarding the properties of the natural world, in his "Letter to the Grand Duchess Cristina" and in other writings. For this mortal sin, he barely escaped being burned alive by his coreligionists. Once more, society tried to make a martyr out of a Galilean.

How has it come about that the application of these prescriptions of Galileo, Descartes, and others—which at first sight seem to be so narrow and restrictive as to hobble the investigation of the natural world—has led instead to the astonishing edifice of knowledge that science has built in only the past 400 years? What accounts for the enormous power of these methods to fathom many of the secrets of the universe that had been hidden for so long? An exploration of these questions and insight into the nature and operations of science result from a comparison of our present views of the structure of the universe (cosmology) with those of the ancient Greeks. This comparison also enables us to appreciate the distinction of the claims of modern science to represent reality, as contrasted to the claims of previous protoscience.

All early civilizations, particularly the Babylonian and the Chinese, made detailed astronomical observations. But the Greeks went on to develop a highly sophisticated cosmology to account for what they observed in the Heavens. In this they were guided by their overarching ideas about the design of the cosmos, by their great interest in geometry, and by common sense. The silent and remote Heavens were taken as perfect and unchanging, the busy planet Earth as imperfect and the seat of all change. As common sense told the Greeks, the Earth was stationary, the center of a finite and relatively small (as compared to our present view) universe. The planets, the moon, the sun, and the stars all moved in circular orbits around the stationary Earth, with the sun and stars making a complete rotation around the Earth once each day. The rotation of the moon and the planets around the Earth had periods different than a single day.

Aristotle, who was interested in the physics of motion, undertook, by means of a physical model of the universe, to explain how all these cosmic movements occurred. There being no such thing as a vacuum allowed in Aristotle's physics, the heavenly bodies were thought to be embedded in concentric spheres around the Earth. These spheres were made of a crystalline transparent form of the fifth element and were connected to one another by swivel joints that joined their respective motions together. The outermost sphere contained all the stars. For a body to be in motion, Aristotle's physics, again based on common sense, required it to be continuously propelled. If such propulsion stopped, the motion stopped. The central idea, then, was that a "Prime Mover" was needed to provide forever the force to turn the outermost sphere; and thus, via the swivel joints, appropriate circular motions were imparted to and maintained for the various planetary and the solar spheres. (At a much later time, when Aristotle's works first became known to the West in the Middle Ages, Thomas Aquinas was moved to equate Aristotle's Prime Mover with the Hebrew-Christian God, thereby happily reconciling Aristotelian cosmic science with Christian doctrine.) Some centuries after Aristotle, when it became clear that simple circular motions of the planets around the Earth did not accord with the observed results, Ptolemy then showed mathematically how to reconcile the data with the concept of perfect circularity by incorporating the idea of epicycles into the motions.

The cosmological views of Aristotle and Ptolemy prevailed for nearly 2,000 years. They were not seriously challenged until Copernicus revived and mathematically enhanced an ancient and discredited heliocentric model that had been devised by Aristarchus around 300 B.C. In his model, the Earth not only moved around a stationary sun once a year but also rotated on its axis once a day. Yet Copernicus could not resolve the common-sense paradoxes that had always been raised to oppose the heliocentric model, including the question of how the Earth could be streaming through space without our sensing that motion, let alone without our being blown into space.

The cosmos constructed by the Greeks was a remarkable edifice, the work of great genius, relying on apparently reasonable postulates and common sense. It is entirely narrow-minded for moderns to think of this cosmology as bizarre or ridiculous just because we now know that it was completely wrong. What *is* important is to understand why, in spite of its illustrious origins, it was wrong. One reason was that Aristotle's common-sense ideas about motion were never seriously tested by experiments and proved to be incorrect. (Common sense, in the absence of supporting experimental evidence, has all too often turned out to be a highly misleading guide to scientific understanding. Common sense, for example, tells us that the sun is rising, when it is really the Earth spinning on its axis that makes it appear so.) Galileo's experimental work established a new law of motion that was later adapted by Newton as the first of his three laws. The new law states that no force is required to propel a body if it is moving at a constant velocity (and, as Newton significantly added, in a straight line). This is in contradiction to Aristotle's views, which stipulated that any motion, including that at constant velocity, requires a force to maintain it. (It is wonderful to contemplate that out of such apparently minor abstractions, a new world was constructed!) This new law removes at one stroke most of the common-sense objections to Copernicus's heliocentric model. It explains why we do not sense the Earth's motion (that is, we feel no force from it), because both the Earth's motion and our motion are close to being at constant velocity. This is similar to our experience of being in an automobile, an airplane, or an elevator: we sense that we are moving only when we accelerate or decelerate (that is, when we *change* velocity); at constant speed, however, we do not feel the motion.

Another reason that the Greek cosmological model was wrong was that the ancients were satisfied with visual observations of the Heavens, which are quite limited. This low-resolution information allowed all kinds of fantasies to be entertained about the heavenly bodies. The Greeks knew about the refraction of light and, as the Chinese did, must have known about the magnifying powers of glass lenses; yet neither the Greeks nor the Chinese ever constructed a telescope. But as soon as Galileo in 1609 trained the primitive, newly invented telescope on the sky, even with its limited magnification, features were readily observed (for example, the moons of Jupiter and the shadows cast by the moon's irregular surface) that upset 2,000 years of geocentric cosmology. A new paradigm of experimentation was ushered in.

By contrast to the means used to construct the cosmology of Aristotle and Ptolemy, modern cosmology has a quite different foundation. It starts with Copernicus, but his heliocentric model is still in the tradition of the ancient Greeks. Although it is a mathematical model, it neither contains new experimental results nor does it address satisfactorily any of the paradoxes of Aristarchus's model. Copernicus's work is crucial not because it *established* the heliocentric model but because it brought back to life in the West the forgotten ancient model as an alternative to the geocentric one. Intuitively, Copernicus sensed that his view was correct,[2] but he could not provide evidence to demonstrate its superiority to the Ptolemaic view. This feat required the new approach espoused by Galileo and Descartes. While the range and scope of scientific study that were marked out initially seemed quite confined, the combination of precise and reductive experimentation with mathematical analysis led, in the hands of Kepler, Galileo, and finally Newton, to a remarkable description of the motions of the planets that fits all the astronomical data. These early mathematical physicists firmly established that the heliocentric model was a more correct description of reality than the geocentric model (after inclusion of the ellipticity of the planetary orbits that Kepler discovered). Furthermore, Newton demolished the ancient Greek view of the complete distinction between the Earth and the Heavens by mathematically proving that gravitational acceleration had the same value for planetary motion as for the free fall of objects on the Earth.

The Newtonian synthesis was the first grand demonstration of the powers of the rational methods of the new science. The excitement that it generated electrified the entire cultural life of the West. It not only brought the scientific study of the natural world into an unaccustomed high prominence, but it also was the intellectual precursor of the entire Enlightenment. It testified to the profundity of the individual human mind when it was free to be rational. The quest for scientific understanding, using the new methods of quantitative experiments and mathematical analysis, started as a trickle and over the next few centuries became a torrent.

A principal reason for this explosive development of science is its *predictive capability*. It turns out that if a theory or a model of an aspect of the world is indeed a close approximation of reality, scientists will inevitably be led to use it to predict new phenomena not previously recognized and to suggest experiments to test the prediction. If these tests confirm the prediction, then the status of the theory or model is greatly advanced. Furthermore, the stress placed on quantitative experimentation has promoted the development of new and ever more precise measurement techniques for all kinds of observations. Quite often, this development has produced more accurate data that could no longer be exactly accounted for by the accepted theory of the phenomenon. In turn, this has encouraged scientists to seek an improved theory that not only better fits the more accurate data but also leads to the prediction of more new phenomena and experiments. In these ways, the progress of scientific understanding is continuous and self-generated. Modern cosmology has resulted from the continuous layering of new experimental data, new ideas, and new theories onto the Newtonian skeleton. By contrast, a theory or a model that does not correctly represent reality reveals its inadequacy by having no predictive capability that can be verified experimentally. Greek cosmology led nowhere scientifically for 2,000 years. It was a dead-end because it was an inadequate version of reality. Modern science is therefore not only self-generating; it is rigorously self-correcting.

As a result of the applications of science, our ideas about the universe and the relation of our Earth to it have undergone an astonishing transformation in the past 400 years, particularly rapidly in the past century. As the millennium arrived, astrophysics and cosmology entered an era of a new burst of productive energy, and hence we await further great strides in determining the structure and evolution of the universe. For the purposes of later discussion, I will briefly summarize the state of modern cosmology here, most of it quite familiar. This understanding has been made possible, in part, by the development of an array of instruments and experimental techniques, starting with the telescope (around 1600) and extending to a wide range of the electromagnetic spectrum: gamma-rays, X-rays, ultraviolet, infrared, microwaves, radio waves, and now space probes. With these methods, a great variety of quite unexpected experimental information about the structure and the evolution of the universe has been obtained. Particularly in the past two centuries, the developing knowledge of physics, especially of the subatomic kind, has helped to interpret this new information.

The Greeks thought, as did virtually everyone until this century, that the extraterrestrial universe was forever unchanging. We now know that the universe is anything but static, although the changes generally occur on a time scale that is extremely long compared to a human life span. The universe as a whole was probably initiated by a localized "big bang" about 15 billion years ago, give or take a few billion. Since then, it has undergone continual expansion. With expansion and cooling, matter (subnuclear particles, and later atomic nuclei) formed, and stars and galaxies arose in the early universe by gravitational attraction of the matter. New stars continue to form, older ones to decay. We now know of the existence of pulsars, quasars, white dwarfs, brown dwarfs, black holes, supernovae, and many other colossal objects in the cosmos that reflect its continual and turbulent evolution. The expanding universe is incredibly vast, distances being measured in light-years. (It takes light, traveling at 186,000 miles per second, about eight minutes to get from the sun to the Earth. The edge of the universe, however, is so far away that it would take about 15 billion years for light from there to reach the Earth!) The universe contains something like 100 billion galaxies, each galaxy consisting of about 100 billion stars. The sun is a relatively recent and not particularly distinguished star, located near the edge of the galaxy known as the Milky Way.

The Earth, far from being the center of the universe, is a minor planet, a dark accretion of matter that orbits around the sun. The sun is about 5 billion years old, and it is estimated that it will continue to shine for another 10 billion years or so. The Earth was formed about 4.5 billion years ago; when its surface cooled down enough, the first stage of single-cell life soon appeared, about 4 billion years ago. Planetary systems around other stars are difficult to detect, but several have recently been discovered, and they are probably quite common in the universe. Forms of life may well exist at many sites in the universe if and where the conditions are favorable.

For almost all of history, humans had not the slightest idea of the immensity of the energies generated by our sun and other stars, let alone the details of their origin. Only some 60 years ago, after the structure of the atomic nucleus was established, did we come to understand that stars are vast furnaces whose hydrogen nuclei continually undergo fusion processes to form helium nuclei; the enormous energy released (according to Einstein's $E = mc^2$) is converted in part to light and heat. Hydrogen and helium are the predominant elements in the universe. But Earth and all of its living creatures contain hardly any helium; instead, they contain many other elements besides hydrogen. Where did these elements come from? When stars finally use up their hydrogen, they decay and disintegrate. As a result, the heavier nuclei of other elements are formed and dispersed into space. Our Earth's and our bodies' contents of carbon, nitrogen, oxygen, phosphorus, and so on—all elements heavier than hydrogen and helium—have arisen from stellar decay that occurred earlier in the evolution of the universe.

The stars, prodigious furnaces that they are, are not the most energetic objects in the universe. They convert only about 1 percent of their mass into energy. In recent years, though, black holes have been discovered. As their name implies, these holes suck in vast quantities of mass that are converted entirely into enormous amounts of energy, as first revealed by their intense radio frequency radiation. Black holes, located near the centers of galaxies, appear to take part in some vast regenerative process in galactic formation.

The differences, then, between the Aristotelian/Ptolemaic view of the cosmos and the modern view reside not only in the utterly dissimilar physical structures inherent in these views but also in the nature of their derivation and, correspondingly, in their relation to reality. The ancient view of the cosmos was simply wrong because it was based on ideas that, however reasonable, were never tested by experiment and turned out to be incorrect. Today's cosmos, established by more sophisticated applications of scientific analysis, is by contrast a close approximation of reality. No future knowledge of the cosmos will change the present picture of a vast, evolving universe with mind-numbing numbers of galaxies, each containing an immense quantity of stars. This view is not a transient one. It does not depend on societal prejudices or cabalistic dogmas, or on the authority vested in superhuman agencies.

Many irrationalists in our society seem unable to grasp these ideas about the established truths of science. God knows why. Apart from the consummate charlatans, some critics seem to think that because science is carried out by ordinary human beings, it should be not only influenced by the egocentricity, obsessions, and failures that characterize most other human endeavors but also determined by them. Influenced, yes; determined, no. The detailed daily exercise of scientific creation is far from a straightforward and totally rational process (see Chapter 11), but the ultimate outcome of these exercises, as refined in the blast furnace of criticism and experimental test, is eventually freed of the impurities introduced by human frailties, which become irrelevant. Other critics of science seem confused by the fact that early in its development a theory or model of a phenomenon may indeed be of only uncertain validity, most often because of a lack of experimental information or theoretical sophistication. If the theory is on the correct track toward a description of reality, however, greater certainty is eventually achieved from new experimental data and from improvements in the theory. Scientists believe—and have not encountered any reason to believe otherwise—that there is only one physical reality, independent of our only incomplete perception and comprehension of it at any time. The progress of science inexorably brings us closer and closer to that reality. Therefore, the initial uncertainty about a theory or a model does not reflect on the much greater reliability that can eventually be attained if the theory is sound.

Scientific ideas change as new information is acquired and new insights are obtained. This is sometimes taken to mean that scientific knowledge is only relative and uncertain, to be blown away by the next icy blast of ideas and replaced by something perhaps unrelated and quite different. According to this interpretation, scientific knowledge has no more claim to truth or validity than any other kind of knowledge—for example, the revealed truth of religion. This view is nonsense. It is a complete distortion of the nature of science and of its continual and systematic development over time. Changes in scientific understanding are not a matter of random fluctuations but are instead systematic and largely linear. They involve a continuous improvement in our knowledge over time; they produce an asymptotically ever more accurate description of reality. In its most firmly established views, that description of reality is virtually certain.

For people who have not had the direct experience of doing scientific research, perhaps a useful, if only rough, analogy to the acquisition of scientific knowledge is the solution of a difficult and tricky crossword puzzle. In the early stages of solving the puzzle, one proceeds by trial and error—making and erasing mistakes, trying to figure out the key to the main idea of the puzzle. Finally, when the puzzle is completed, one is satisfied that the solution is clearly correct, apart perhaps from a few letters that may be wrong, and is the only solution possible. Why? What makes us feel certain about the solution? It is not only because the words all fit together precisely but also because many of them, in retrospect, reveal the unity of the design. No resort to any gibberish words has been made. Yet there are no specific rules by which one can tell that the solution is correct; and, until the answer is published the next week, one is presumably not certain. Nevertheless, we know instinctively when we have correctly solved the puzzle, and so we proceed to the next one, confident that the correct solution cannot be significantly different. Science on a grander scale is like that. All the many pieces of the scientific puzzle, all the experimental facts, eventually fit so neatly into the proposed theory or mechanism, and the end result makes such complete sense, that a capable scientist is almost certain about the conclusion, even if there are no simple rules by which to affirm it. We can be confident that no entirely unrelated solution is going to be devised in the future.

When Albert Einstein published his theory of general relativity in 1916, he radically changed the views of space and time that had been taken for granted for millennia and that were central to Newtonian physics. Instead of independent and absolute Newtonian space and time, relativity shows that space and time are interdependent and relative. This is sometimes erroneously taken to mean that, with Einstein's utterly revolutionary theory, Newtonian concepts were discarded as completely wrong (as Aristotelian concepts had previously been rejected as wrong); therefore, by extrapolating from this notion, one might claim that all scientific knowledge is only relative and transient, vulnerable to replacement by a random burst of new ideas. As Einstein himself stated, however, his theory did not represent a complete discontinuity but rather was a natural extension and continuation of the scientific process. What is more, Newtonian physics, in contrast to Aristotle's, is not wrong but is incomplete, applying satisfactorily only to bodies moving slowly compared to the speed of light and positing gravity as an ad hoc phenomenon. General relativity is the more complete theory, and it also explains gravitation.

Scientific truth relies for its adoption on persuasion by the weight of unbiased and reproducible evidence—not on persuasion by reports of occult miracles or the threat of the rack. There will always be some who remain unpersuaded by a generally accepted scientific truth. They are not ostracized by the scientific community; rather, their views are often published and seriously considered. When such skepticism is based on reason, it can generate new insights and knowledge. But when it is irrational, it will ultimately be consigned to oblivion. No one will remember Trofim Lysenko 50 years from now, but the memory of Gregor Mendel and Charles Darwin will remain vital for a long time to come.[3]

For rationalists who are not scientists and cannot judge for themselves the merits of the latest scientific experiment or theory, it is probably best to await a consensus view of the experiment or theory by scientists who are specialists in the particular area involved. Scientists are usually highly conservative, reluctant to accept new ideas unless those ideas are satisfactorily verified, so the ultimate consensus of scientists is usually reliable. What appears in the better textbooks is ordinarily backed by such a consensus.

The advances in cosmology and astrophysics singled out in this chapter are representative of similarly great achievements in the other physical sciences as well: in many other branches of physics, in chemistry, and in geology, for example. In the twentieth century, astonishing and revolutionary insights have been produced in all these sciences. The nature of the universe, though, which is the subject of cosmology, is distinctive because it is so directly relevant to our views of the world we live in, much more so than these other physical sciences. So I will not address these other advances but instead will turn directly to modern biology, that other science most relevant to humans.

CHAPTER 4

Modern Biology and the Response to Vitalism

While cosmology generally concerns matters remote from our everyday experience, biology, the science of life, speaks directly to us. It says who we are, how we function, and how we came to be. It stands to reason that biology, and human biology in particular, should have great relevance for understanding the operations of human society. This is the message of the field of sociobiology and its principal champion, E. O. Wilson. The main problem with the application of biological science to the social sciences is that human biology itself is still new and relatively unexplored. Many of its paradigms are of recent vintage and have not yet been widely diffused to the public. Furthermore, the stakes involved for various elements of society are high. The scientific knowledge of human beings can be expected to encounter considerable resistance if it conflicts with the unscientific beliefs and practices of powerful institutions in society such as religion, the law, and the academy. Nevertheless, sociobiology is here to stay, inevitably growing more and more influential as the science of biology continues to yield new insights into human beings and their behavior. It is a primary theme of this book to encourage bringing biological sciences to bear on human affairs.

Although the study of biology goes back a long way in history, it is particularly in the past 50 years that modern biology has firmly established a new understanding of ourselves, and we are still only at the beginning of this revolution. Modern biology is the extension of the scientific methods of Galileo and others to the realm of living things. Prior to these insights, biology was primarily a descriptive and phenomenological science, mostly concerned with natural history and physiology, eventually leading to cell theory and to the grand synthesis of Darwinian evolution. Modern biology had to await the knowledge of physics and chemistry that came to flower in the first part of the twentieth century before the complex molecular structure and function of living systems could be elucidated at the most fundamental level. Therefore, knowledge of the physics and chemistry of inanimate matter was well established before modern biology evolved.

The axiomatic basis of modern biology is that living systems must at all times conform to the universal laws and operations of physics and chemistry. They cannot transcend them, as, for example, by miracles of superhuman or divine intervention.

An axiom cannot be proved to be correct. Its validity is a matter of long experience and allows for no credible exceptions. It is axiomatic that the sun will "rise" tomorrow and the next day, but it cannot be proved beforehand. It is a matter of long experience without exceptions. Myths or miracles that suggest the contrary, such as that of the unfortunate Phaëthon, do not constitute credible exceptions. That an axiom cannot be proved, however, does not necessarily detract from its reliability. Do you entertain the slightest doubt that the sun will rise tomorrow?

In earlier times, most thoughtful people considered life, especially human life, to be too extraordinary and too intricate to be constrained like mere dust by the ordinary laws of physics and chemistry. Not comprehending modern biology, many in our times still consider this to be so. In the population at large today, most believe in a divine Creation of human life (91 percent of Americans, according to the Gallup poll cited in Chapter 1). Even though many rationalists think that it is dead, Vitalism, the ancient doctrine that life transcends ordinary physics and chemistry, including a belief in a divine Creation and the existence of a life following death, still holds sway over the Western world. Anyone who believes in an afterlife is a Vitalist (see Chapter 5). Yet everything we have learned in biology accords with the view that, mechanistically, life involves nothing beyond a special and highly intricate organization of inanimate matter, so structured and self-programmed as to continually take in energy (ultimately derived from the light energy of the sun) and convert much of it into order (that is, reducing entropy) and function, including reproduction. The property that characterizes living systems is that they are *never* in thermodynamic equilibrium. Equilibrium is death. Life is governed mainly by the principles of irreversible thermodynamics, whereas the inanimate world generally conforms to the laws of reversible thermodynamics.[1] Life is therefore a most unusual state of matter, and, while magnificently complex, it appears to have required nothing outside the realm of physics and chemistry to have evolved in the first place or to have maintained and greatly elaborated itself over the following 4 billion years of evolution.

How do living systems work? Once encountered, the principles are simple, and anyone can comprehend them. The details are what is complicated, but we will not need them here. Living systems are remarkably versatile chemical machines capable of using their special chemistry to perform numerous critical functions. To carry out these functions, all organisms require the uptake of energy. Fairly early in the evolution of life, mechanisms evolved to use the only large, uniformly spread, and steady source of energy available on earth, sunlight. Light energy is taken up by the living systems that can perform the process known as photosynthesis, which include the photosynthetic bacteria and algae, phytoplankton, and almost all members of the plant kingdom. Photosynthesis is one of the great marvels of life. A plant snatches from the air the simple molecule carbon dioxide (CO_2), which is present in only a small percentage in the atmosphere; it takes from the ground the most common of all molecules, water (H_2O); it bonds to bacteria that capture the simple molecule nitrogen (N_2) from the atmosphere and convert it to small nitrogen-containing molecules; it picks up a few other elements such as phosphorus and sulfur; it absorbs and directs the energy of sunlight[2]—and, presto, from these the plant then makes all of the giant molecules, the proteins, the DNA, all the cellulose and other structures of its cells, everything it requires to remain alive and grow, *and*, in the same process, it produces from H_2O the oxygen (O_2) in the atmosphere that all animal life needs to survive.

Photosynthesis provides the means to construct the entire cathedral of plant life, starting from the sand and water it takes to make the necessary bricks and mortar. Virtually all life depends on it. Photosynthetic species utilize the chemical energy that they have converted from light energy and have stored as sugars and other substances in their tissues. All other species on earth get the energy they need by feeding on these primary energy transducers. Or they eat other organisms that have eaten the plants. That is ultimately why, in the event of a widespread nuclear war, all life would likely be exterminated, because the enormous clouds of dust and debris that would cover the earth for months afterward would blot out the sunlight necessary to sustain life. The radiation from the nuclear blasts wouldn't help either.

What do organisms do with the chemical energy they derive from the food they eat? An incredible number of things. They use the energy to produce other chemical molecules they need to grow and maintain their body structures, to reproduce their kind, to receive and process sensory signals from the environment, to move their body parts, and so forth.

In only the short span of the past few decades, chemists and biologists have learned a great deal about how these functions are carried out. Living organisms accomplish all of their multitudinous sensory and physical activities by relying on—along with the ordinary small molecules of chemistry, such as the sugars and amino acids—giant chemical molecules that are unique to life (such as the proteins, RNA, and DNA). But life is more than a random collection of crucial molecules. The living state is, above all, a matter of organization and structure, of order imposed on disorder. This organization takes place at several levels of size and complexity. Thus, the proteins, RNA, DNA, and other giant linear molecules of living systems are not just shapeless, loosely arranged strings like individual strands of cooked spaghetti; instead, each is constrained by its internal chemical forces to fold into a unique and specific shape, or conformation, that is crucial for its chemical function. At the next level of organization, these intricately shaped molecules are not simply thrown together but are organized inside microscopically small units called cells. Each cell is enveloped by an extremely thin but remarkably sturdy membrane that separates the constituents inside from the ones outside; this permits a highly selective molecular import of nutrients into, and export of poisons out of, the cell. The next level of organization requires that cells arrange themselves inside tissues and organs. Then the organism develops from the programmed assemblage and proper placement of the tissues and organs inside an appropriate outer shell. Finally, at the highest level, organisms of different species, having arisen by the processes of natural selection, are collected and segregated into biological and social communities in the biosphere.

The uniquely biological molecules, the proteins, RNA, and DNA, and their organization into cells and higher structures, are clearly the keys to the operations of life. The branch of science that investigates them, molecular biology, has made remarkable progress, especially considering what it has already accomplished in its 50-year lifetime. Molecular biology, as complex as it is, is enormously simplified as a consequence of the evolutionary basis of living systems. Because of evolution, the immense varieties of living forms display a striking similarity among the many kinds of molecules and functions that they share. For example, the protein molecule rhodopsin in the eye of an insect, which captures the photon of light in vision, is closely similar but not identical to the rhodopsin that performs the same function in the human eye. What is learned at the molecular and cellular level of simple organisms is often transferable to humans.[3]

Proteins are the cell's chemical work horses. Because each kind of protein generally does only one thing chemically (see Chapter 8), a great many kinds are necessary to carry out all of the cell's many chemical functions. There are between 50,000 and 100,000 different kinds of proteins in humans, each performing one of the multiple steps of energy reception and conversion, molecular synthesis and breakdown, or one of the many other processes required to maintain life. At present we are familiar with only a few thousand of these proteins. All of the protein molecules are different but are constructed on the same general design. They all are built up by the chemical linkage of only 20 different building blocks, the amino acids. Each kind of protein molecule has its own linear order, or sequence, of 20 amino acids successively chemically linked to its neighbor amino acids. This is roughly analogous to having a vast dictionary of words all derived from the same 26 letters of the alphabet. Whereas single words rarely have more than 15 letters, however, single kinds of protein molecules can have hundreds or thousands of the 20 amino acid building blocks strung in a chain. The linear order of the building blocks is characteristic of a certain protein molecule. This sequence determines exactly how the molecule folds up in three dimensions to give the molecule a particular complex shape; and, as mentioned earlier, it is this special shape for each kind of protein molecule that consigns to it a particular chemical function. (See Appendix A for a more detailed explanation.)

A large fraction of proteins are enzymes, which are molecules designed by evolution to make each kind of enzyme capable of accelerating a particular chemical reaction rapidly at body temperature. In the absence of the enzyme, the same chemical reaction requires a much higher temperature to occur. The principle of enzyme action is simple; the chemical mechanisms are marvelously complex and ingenious (see Appendix A). Life as we know it is inconceivable without protein enzymes. They are the catalytic converters of living systems.

What about DNA? To understand the crucial role of DNA in the chemistry of life, we must first come to grips with some of the facts of how hereditary characteristics are transmitted from parent to offspring in all living systems. Early humans must already have been aware of hereditary transmission because their children often looked strikingly like one of the mates and quite different from other, unrelated people. But remarkably little progress was made in understanding the phenomenon until Gregor Mendel in 1865 performed his quantitative experiments on the inheritance of individual traits such as flower color in hybrids of ordinary garden peas. From his experiments, he realized that hereditary transmission takes place by way of previously unsuspected units, particulate structures that remain intact during such transmission. These structures ultimately became known as genes—and hence the science of heredity is called genetics.

At this early stage, it was thought that each trait was specified by one gene. Each parental gene not only must be retained by the parent but also must be transmitted to the offspring. Each parental gene must therefore be replicated exactly, and the copy passed intact to the offspring. What this means at the molecular level is that whatever the chemical molecule that constitutes each gene, it has to be faithfully replicated in the process of reproduction; that is, the replicate must be strung together chemically so as to be an exact copy of the original. Chemists, confronted with this problem of molecular replication in its abstract form, were quite mystified by how it might occur. There was no precedent for such precise copying in ordinary chemistry.

To understand the basis for hereditary transmission, it was first necessary to identify the chemical substance constituting each gene and then to determine how it was faithfully replicated. After much investigation, it was finally proved in the 1940s that the chemical substance of the gene is the giant molecule deoxyribonucleic acid (DNA). DNA molecules are all long linear chains constructed by the successive chemical linkage of four building blocks, called nucleotides, which are designated A, G, C, and T. The key to the structure of the DNA molecule, and to its function in chemical reproduction, was eventually figured out: it is that A and T have a strong affinity for each other, as do G and C. Now, an individual chain of DNA has its own linear order, or sequence, of the four linked building blocks. Part of this sequence might, for instance, be the following:

$$\rightarrow \;\ldots\text{A–G–C–C–G–T–C–A–G–G–C–A–}\ldots \;\rightarrow$$

where the solid dashes denote the linkage between the successive nucleotides, and the arrows indicate the direction of the linear chain. In 1953, James Watson and Francis Crick realized that the affinities of A for T and of G for C dictated that the DNA chains would not be like individual coils of spaghetti, but instead would adopt a fairly rigid and rod-like *duplex* structure arranged as an anti-parallel double helix, in which the sequence just shown, for example, would be paired to its so-called complement, thus:

$$\rightarrow \;\ldots\text{–A–G–C–C–G–T–C–A–G–G–C–A–}\ldots \;\rightarrow$$
$$\;\;\;\;\;\;\;\;\;\vdots\;\vdots\;\vdots\;\vdots\;\vdots\;\vdots\;\vdots\;\vdots\;\vdots\;\vdots\;\vdots\;\vdots$$
$$\leftarrow \;\ldots\text{–T–C–G–G–C–A–G–T–C–C–G–T–}\ldots \;\leftarrow$$

This structure immediately suggests schematically how the chemical replication of DNA occurs. The process involves separating the two complementary chains of the parental double helix and then laying down, one nucleotide after the other, a new complementary chain along each of the two parental chains (see Figure 1). The result of such an operation is the formation of two double helices that are identical to the original parental DNA, each double helix now containing one chain of the parental DNA. This process, called replication, is carried out with the aid of special protein enzymes. And DNA replication is the simple and beautiful chemical secret behind the reproduction of life and the transmission of heredity. Take a few minutes to savor the fact that this secret you now share is one that all the scientific geniuses of yesteryear, the Aristotles, Newtons, and Einsteins, did not have the good fortune to know.

But why is it necessary to replicate and pass on the DNA? What essential function does the DNA perform in living systems? These questions were answered in the late 1950s. The principal function of the DNA is to encode the information for the production of all the many kinds of proteins in an organism; that is, to encode for all the linear sequences of the amino acid building blocks of each kind of protein molecule. The molecular decoding of DNA is called translation, since it achieves the conversion from one linear "language" (the nucleotide sequence) to another co-linear one (the amino acid sequence).

In a remarkably short time in the 1960s, the details of the translation process were worked out. In the DNA, a particular sequence of three successive nucleotides, a so-called triplet codon, encodes for a particular amino acid and no other (see Appendix B). This genetic code is virtually identical for all life forms,

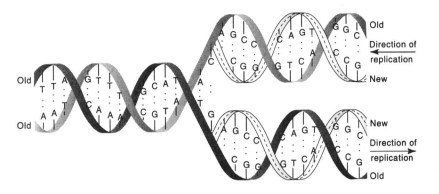

Figure 1. A schematic intermediate stage during the replication of DNA. The still-unreplicated DNA is on the left. The two strands of the double helix have been separated on the right, and two new complementary strands (dashed ribbon) have been laid down one base at a time on each of the old strands. The four bases A, G, C, and T, protruding from the backbones of the strands, are specifically paired (A–T and G–C) in the double helices. Note that the two replicates on the right are identical to each other as well as to the region of the old DNA from which they were formed.

from bacteria to human beings. Utilizing a marvelous piece of molecular machinery called a ribosome, itself constructed from RNA and about 80 different kinds of protein molecules, a transcript of the DNA (called messenger RNA) is fed into the ribosome and is read continuously three nucleotides at a time. The corresponding linear sequence of the amino acids of that protein molecule is then fed out of the ribosome from one end to the other, and one copy after another. For every kind of protein molecule, there is a corresponding stretch of DNA. And this is the modern definition of a gene at the molecular level: it is a linear stretch of DNA whose nucleotide sequence encodes the linear amino acid sequence of a specific protein molecule. Because the proteins carry out most of the chemical and functional aspects of life, these processes are encoded in the DNA and are transmitted hereditarily when the DNA is faithfully replicated and passed on to the next generation.

All kinds of biological phenomena are now for the first time capable of being understood in terms of this DNA/protein functional relationship. Consider, for example, the molecular nature of a mutation, defined as a change in an organism that is hereditarily transmitted. The simplest kind of mutation (referred to as a point mutation) occurs when one nucleotide in a DNA sequence is chemically changed to another—say, an A is converted to a G by an agent such as ultraviolet radiation from the sun or chemical attack within the body by a chemical free radical. This change clearly produces an altered triplet codon, which may now be the codon for an amino acid different from that encoded by the original triplet. As a result, the protein defined by the mutated gene would now have a different amino acid inserted at the corresponding site in its linear chain. This altered protein might now exhibit either the same or an altered function compared to the protein defined by the nonmutated gene. The altered function might change one or more of the characteristic traits of the organism determined by the protein. This change, if it occurred in the germ-line cells (see Appendix D), would now be hereditary, passed on from one generation to the next by the process of DNA replication during reproduction.

As a result of such mutational events occurring at random sites in the DNA in individuals of a species, the species as a whole accumulates alternative forms of a given gene (called alleles), which are distributed among the members of the species. A major consequence is that no two human beings, except for identical twins, are genetically identical. Each of us may have a number of slightly different variants among our 50,000 to 100,000 genes that are allelic forms of the corresponding genes of our neighbors. As a result, the total DNA of one human can be as much as 0.1 percent different chemically from that of another, as compared to the 1 to 2 percent difference between human and chimpanzee DNA. These differences have many crucial consequences for human beings and their societies, a subject I'll take up later. For now, it is sufficient to note that this diversity of human DNA is the basis for most of the physical differences that distinguish each of us. It also allows for the powerful forensic technique of DNA fingerprinting. Genetic diversity is also ultimately responsible for the rejection of transplanted tissues donated by one unrelated individual to another. We continually encounter such genetic diversity in our lives.

This molecular information also gives us a clearer view of the mechanisms behind Darwinian evolution. The diversity of living things has always been evident to humans, even if its enormity was not appreciated early on. (If all living species had been created at one stroke by a divine act, it would have indeed been difficult to get a male and a female of each and every species aboard Noah's Ark, since we now estimate that there are probably tens of millions of living species on Earth. Furthermore, we hear no mention of Noah and his sons collecting all the millions of species of bacteria and other microscopic organisms to keep them from extinction by the Flood.) The great organizing idea of biological diversity, the Darwinian theory of evolution, has been extended by recent knowledge about DNA, genes, and proteins. Modern evolution holds that all living species, including humans, arose successively over billions of years by gene mutations and natural selection from simpler forms of life that go back to single-celled, bacteria-like organisms—and even earlier, to still more primitive forms that have long since become extinct. Although many details of the conditions in which evolutionary changes arose are lost in shadowy time, there is now no scientific doubt that the evolution of life forms did occur over billions of years and that the human species is its most recent prodigy. The convergent experimental information derived from diverse sciences—geology, paleontology, physiology, anatomy, biochemistry, molecular biology, and genetics—makes the theory of evolution as assuredly correct as almost anything else we know (not much less certain than 2 plus 2 equals 4). The efforts of creationists and other irrationalists to picture evolutionary doctrine as not scientifically established are without merit.

The molecular basis for evolution is that the infrequent occurrence of one or another kind of mutation in a stretch of DNA in germ-line cells may result in an alteration of the amino acid sequence of the protein encoded by that DNA (gene). If this change in the protein creates a severe enough loss of chemical function, the organism may then die early in its life, before it has an opportunity to reproduce and pass on the defective mutated gene to its progeny. The deleterious mutation is thus eliminated. By contrast, if a DNA mutation now codes for an altered protein with a significantly enhanced function that improves the health or reproductive vigor of the organism, that individual will enjoy a selective reproductive advantage over the nonmutated individuals of the species. The mutated gene may then be retained as part of the pool of genes of that species. (How such processes lead to speciation, the generation of new species during evolution, is reviewed later in this chapter.)

How did life on Earth originate? Modern biologists insist that there is no necessity, nor any rational basis, for the religious doctrine that it was created by a divine act. Most probably, life began spontaneously on the primitive Earth soon after the planet was formed, by a combination of chemical and physical processes (although we may never know exactly how). This would have been some 4 billion years ago, when the Earth's surface had cooled sufficiently after its formation about 4.5 billion years ago. The genus *Homo* arose only about 3 to 5 million years ago, from hominid ancestors that in turn arose from an ancestral species held in common with the chimpanzee. Reflecting this ancestral relationship, the chemical structure of human DNA differs from chimpanzee DNA by less than 2 percent; in fact, many of the genes from the two species, and therefore the proteins they encode, are identical. The DNA of all other species shows differences greater than 2 percent from human DNA, in proportion to their remoteness from humans in evolution and as a result of the net accumulation of mutations during evolutionary time.

Armed with this knowledge of the molecular processes of life, modern biologists have achieved a detailed understanding of how many of the remarkable phenomena of life work—that is, how the incredibly complex activities of life are carried out chemically and mechanically, without requiring a divine design or intervention. I will now describe some of these phenomena, to illustrate this modern perspective as well as for other purposes.

But first, one more molecular fact. Whereas the molecules of the different kinds of proteins each contain two free ends (see Appendix B), meaning that the molecules are separate entities, the corresponding stretches of DNA (the genes) are not separate but are connected together in long chains called chromosomes. The

DNA is wrapped in folds of specific types of proteins in the chromosome. Humans possess 23 pairs of microscopically distinguishable chromosomes. Given the total number of genes (50,000 to 100,000), on average each chromosome may thus contain on the order of 2,500 to 5,000 different genes strung together in a particular linear arrangement. The significance of this is that when the DNA is replicated, each entire chromosome is doubled; the transmission of genes from parent to offspring occurs via intact chromosomes.

The replication of DNA and the duplication of chromosomes are the primal and essential events in the reproduction of life, but they are not the whole story. The single cell is the most primitive form of life (see Chapter 8), and the reproduction of life involves the reproduction of single cells. Although most biologists believe that the earliest forms of life arose *de novo*, life as we now know it arises only from already established life, by the growth and duplication of living cells. How do cells reproduce? By duplication. Many rounds of cell duplication constitute the main process that produces the often enormous growth of an organism after it is conceived and until it reaches maturity. A human being starts out as a single cell (called a zygote) and finally contains many thousand billions of cells. The initial zygote results from the fusion of a single sperm cell from the male with a single egg cell from the female. In the zygote, the 23 chromosomes from the sperm cell are mixed with the corresponding 23 chromosomes from the egg; each zygote thus contains one pair of each type of chromosome, and therefore two copies of each type of gene, one from the mother and one from the father. To go from the zygote to the adult involves a long succession of cell divisions, in which single cells divide in two by the process of asexual reproduction.

The crucial molecular events in asexual reproduction are, first, the faithful replication of the DNA in all of the 46 chromosomes in a parental cell, which produces two identical copies of each of the 46 chromosomes; and, second, the precise partitioning of one copy of each of the 46 chromosomes into the two daughter cells (in a marvelous sequence of micromechanical events called mitosis; see Appendix C). The two daughter cells accordingly have exactly the same complement of genes that the parental cell possessed. Therefore, every cell in an adult human body possesses exactly the same genes as every other (with a few exceptions, including germ cells), and the same as those deposited in the original fertilized egg: one copy of each of the 23 chromosomes from the father and one copy of the 23 from the mother.

This fact immediately raises a major question. We know that the human body contains many distinct kinds of cells with different characteristics and functions—liver cells, muscle cells, skin cells, nerve cells, and so on. If, as a result of the many rounds of asexual reproduction that produce the adult, every cell in the body has the identical collection of genes, how can so many of the body's cells be so different from one another? The answer, at least in principle, turns out to be straightforward, and exceedingly important. Each gene can be in one of two alternative states: "on" or "off," as determined by the molecular interaction between the gene's DNA and specific proteins called regulators. In the on state, a gene can be decoded in order to permit the synthesis of the protein that it specifically encodes; in the off state, the gene is blocked by its regulator proteins and cannot be decoded. In liver, muscle, skin, and nerve cells, different sets of genes are turned on, and others are turned off. Therefore, although each of these cell types has the identical set of genes, they each contain a different set of proteins. These proteins give the individual cell types their special characteristics and functions. This phenomenon of cell diversification within a single organism is called differentiation.

Whereas the duplication of cells during an organism's growth is by asexual reproduction, the generation of whole new organisms such as humans generally occurs by sexual reproduction. In the long evolution of life, asexual reproduction preceded sexual. The latter process was eventually selected in evolution because of the advantages it conferred on the survival of a species. But sexual reproduction did not effectively take over until the bacteria-like cell evolved into the much larger eukaryotic cell that constitutes a now separate realm. The critical cellular processes in the course of sexual reproduction are collectively called meiosis, which is confined to a few sets of differentiated cells, the germ-cell line: one in the male, and another in the female. The end result of meiosis is a set of sperm cells in the male and a set of egg cells in the female, each of which in the human contains only one copy of each of the 23 kinds of chromosomes. (For the micromechanics of meiosis, see Appendix D.) A crucial aspect of meiosis is that the one chromosome of each kind that winds up in a given sperm cell is derived at *random* from either the father or the mother of the male; and, likewise, in each egg cell of the female one chromosome of each kind is derived at random from the female's mother or father. The effect is to produce a vast host of sperm cells in each of which 50 percent of the chromosomes (and hence 50 percent of the genes) are derived from the male's father and 50 percent from the male's mother. If you remember that the same genes in any two chromosomes may be alleles of one another, it then follows that each sperm cell of one individual male is genetically different from every other because each of its 23 chromosomes is randomly derived either from the father or from the mother of the male. Likewise for the egg cells of an individual female.

This is why the several offspring of a union between the same male and female are not genetically identical to one another, unless they are identical twins. Each sibling arises from the fusion of a genetically unique sperm cell from the same father with a genetically unique egg cell from the same mother to produce a genetically unique fertilized egg containing 46 chromosomes. By contrast, if new whole organisms were to be produced by asexual reproduction, they would all be genetically identical to one another and to the parent. The latter process is what the cloning of organisms is all about—and it is how bacteria generally reproduce.

The crucial purpose served by sexual reproduction, therefore, is to produce great genetic diversity among the different individuals of a single species. All humans are genetically closely similar to one another, which is what makes them all human; but no two are genetically identical, except for identical twins. This is why the physical appearances of two identical twins are so difficult to distinguish, whereas most humans are readily recognized as physically unique. The uniqueness of each human extends to all other genetically determined characteristics. Genetic diversity is consequently directly and crucially involved in human affairs, even though many of us may be largely unaware of the extent to which this is so.

Why, you might ask, is genetic diversity so important to living systems that evolution has developed and selected such a complex process as sexual reproduction to achieve it? It is because the selective advantage conferred by genetic diversity has been of paramount importance to the survival of species throughout evolutionary history. Confronted with a new and lethal bacterial, viral, or fungal infection, for example, or a severe change in the environment, many individuals of a species will die. Yet some others may possess alleles of genes that render them resistant to the disease or environmental change. These individuals will survive to reproduce and maintain the species. A species whose members are all genetically identical clones of one another could become extinct under such conditions. We see this genetic diversity operating today with HIV infections of human beings. Most humans appear to be lethally susceptible to this virus, but a fraction of the population, although exposed to HIV, appears to be completely resistant to it. This resistance is most probably conferred by currently unknown allelic genes (or gene) possessed by certain people that differ from the ones in the population at large.

VITALISTIC ARGUMENTS AND THEIR REBUTTAL

The Thrust Toward Increased Consciousness and Complexity of Life

Questions and arguments have been raised over the years to support a Vitalistic view of life, the view that life must transcend the merely mechanical laws and operations of chemistry and physics. One such Vitalistic contention concerns the differing degrees of complexity within the chain of living things, from bacteria at one end to humans at the other. Even if we accept evolution, the argument goes, why should living forms have become more complicated, and ever more mentally capable, except by a divine thrust toward perfection? Why didn't life remain at the level of the highly functional and very diversified bacteria, as indeed it apparently did for the first 2 billion years of life on Earth? Even if we interpret Biblical Genesis in an allegorical rather than in a literal sense, the ultimate preeminence of the genus *Homo* was part of God's design, so the Vitalists argue. They contend that humans are not just the most recently arrived among the Earth's inhabitants; rather, God saw to it that the human race was the final and crowning form of life, created in His image and the most nearly perfect, to be given dominion over all the Earth and its inhabitants. This argument has impressed and deeply influenced a great many intelligent people over the centuries.

The straightforward and mechanistic answer of modern biology to this Vitalist argument has become clear in recent decades. No external agent, no deity, was required to generate the divergence and growing complexity of living forms during evolution. More complex functionality arose spontaneously, as a consequence of infrequently occurring mechanisms operating initially at the level of the genes. One of these mechanisms is called gene duplication. Briefly, this is the way it works. During the process of meiosis (Appendix D provides a primer on this phenomenon), there is an early stage when the DNA of the 46 chromosomes of the germ-line cell—the 23 from the individual's father and the 23 from the mother—is replicated. This replication creates four strands of each type of chromosome, with all four lined up in parallel and remaining connected to one another (a tetrad, as depicted in stage *b* in Figure D, p. 209). In this state, they can often undergo a genetic process called crossing-over (see Figure E, p. 211). In two of the four strands (one from the father and one from the mother), the double helix of DNA is cut, and then the strands cross over and are rejoined. If the respective sites of cleavage on the two strands are not perfectly matched to one another, such unequal crossing-over can result in one strand with *two* adjacent copies of the same gene, while the other strand is left with *no* copies of that gene. The first of the two strands now contains a gene duplication that can be stably transmitted during meiosis and, eventually, reproduction. In principle, such occasional unequal crossing-over events can occur anywhere along a chromosome; hence gene duplications can gradually arise for any of a large number of genes.

Why should something as exotic as gene duplication be of so much interest? Ordinarily, if a single copy of a gene is present on a chromosome, natural selection constrains it from undergoing significant mutation because the protein product that it encodes might lose or greatly alter its important chemical function in the cell. (Thus, the individual germ-line cell left without any copy of the gene after unequal crossing-over [see Figure E, p. 211] will lose a vital function and will likely die. *Decreasing* complexity is therefore generally selected *against*.) If a chromosome contains a gene duplication after unequal crossing-over, however, one copy of that gene is free to undergo substantial mutations, so long as the other gene copy remains mostly unchanged and continues to encode its minimally altered and essential protein product. Hence the gene copy that is free to mutate can eventually undergo enough mutations to generate an altered protein with potentially new and useful functions. (The mostly unaltered gene copy retains the original protein function.) If these new functions are of reproductive advantage, the organism with the mutated duplicated gene, accompanied by the only minimally altered original gene, will be selected for survival.

It is evident that the accumulation of enough gene duplications and subsequent mutations of one copy of each of the duplicated genes can cause the natural selection of individuals and species that not only differ from their ancestors but also are more complex genetically and functionally. With more genes (more protein-encoding DNA per cell), they can do more complex and often advantageous things. Humans, for instance, have between 50,000 and 100,000 protein-encoding DNA genes, compared to only a few thousand for most bacteria. This increase did not arise by the *de novo* production of new DNA, but from previously existing DNA by mechanisms such as gene duplication. In addition, other genetic mechanisms can heighten genetic complexity and speciation, including the occasional duplication of entire chromosomes and the excision and reinsertion elsewhere within the genome of genetic elements known as "jumping genes." The evolution of more complex life forms has been a slow, self-generating, spontaneous, and continuing mutational process, not one that requires any direction by a supernatural being.

This is not to say that the history of all the genetic events of evolution is understood. In fact, as yet, knowledge of the precise course of speciation is only rudimentary, and it may always remain so. In particular, the details of the remarkable evolution of modern humans, with their extraordinary brains, remain a subject of intense scientific investigation and debate. Nevertheless, no insuperable obstacles have been raised to the principle that modern humans are only among the most recent progeny of the long history of the natural evolution of complexity and consciousness on the planet Earth.

A few clarifying thoughts about species are in order. All members of a species are characterized by a set of genes, around which some allelic variations create genetic diversity. The members of a species form a pseudo-clone; their characteristic genes make the members extremely like one another, while the allelic forms of these genes create diversity among the members. All humans clearly differ from all chimpanzees; the members of each species form a pseudo-clone. Within each species, allelic variants of characteristic genes enable humans to be readily differentiated by other humans, even if they cannot easily distinguish between different chimps. Because species distinctiveness would be lost by cross-breeding among them, species are maintained by the evolutionary development of molecular restrictions on the cross-fertilization of the sperm and eggs of different species, by attractive mechanisms that ensure selective mating only within a species, and also by geographic isolation.

The Argument from Design

Another commonly adduced Vitalistic argument is the one from design. Just look at the gleaming forms and beautiful symmetries of living things, contrasted with the often shapeless or jagged structures of the inanimate world. How can such immaculate form and symmetry arise from the operations of the blind forces of chemistry and physics? How could the precision and near-perfect reproducibility that characterize the developmental process, whereby a highly intricate and adept adult organism is conjured up time and again from a microcosmic speck, a single fertilized egg cell, be simply a spontaneous occurrence? Living things are the embodiment of order existing in an inanimate world characterized by the drive toward disorder. How can that order arise from disorder except by the act of a Generator of Organized Design? Clocks do not self-assemble spontaneously; they require a clockmaker to construct them, so the argument goes.

What biologists have learned in the past three decades is that the design of living things, even to the most minute detail, is specified and programmed by genes. Life's designs spontaneously result from the actions of proteins encoded by hundreds of developmental genes that are successively turned on or off (as explained on p. 55) at certain times and locations within the developing embryo. If any of these developmentally important genes are defective or missing, corresponding changes arise in the body plan. All these actions have been uncovered from research on many kinds of species. Populations of a species have been made to undergo random mutations, and rare mutants were detected that showed some kind of significant change in the normal body plan. The corresponding change in the genes of that organism was then tracked down. In 1972, Edward Lewis carried out pioneering studies of this type with the *Drosophila* fruit fly, a very favorable organism for genetic study. In one subsequent and remarkable instance, a fly was produced that had a fully developed leg growing out of each side of its head. It was then shown that this fantastic change in the fly's body plan had resulted from a mutation in just a single gene.

The subsequent elaborations of these experiments demonstrate the multigenic control of the many individual bodily features of plant and animal development.[4] No external agency, no deity, is required to explain the design of living things. The genes involved in development arose early in the evolution of life, and they became more ramified and complex as later species evolved. It is easy to recognize the strong chemical homologies (that is, the relatedness of the sequences of the DNA nucleotides) retained among these developmental genes throughout evolution. Many developmental genes of humans are similar, but not identical, to those of the *Drosophila* fruit fly, for example.

The great awe that is appropriately inspired by the meticulously regulated growth and organization of living things and their resultant often exquisite forms is in no way diminished by these findings of modern biology. Biologists are more dazzled by these phenomena the more they learn about them. Awe and a sense of majesty remain powerful even as ignorance and mystical notions are overcome. Vitalism, which is mysticism, has no bearing on the design of living things.

In a related context, the structures of the bodies of living organisms are not related arbitrarily to one another but are obliged to conform to the laws of physics that are applied to inanimate structures in the science of mechanical engineering. The relative sizes, structures, and arrangements of bones, joints, and all other parts of animal bodies; the organization of structure in giant trees that gives them their strength and stability; and so on—all are clearly constrained by the same principles of mathematics and physics that engineers use to construct our machines, bridges, and skyscrapers. This congruity has important implications for evolution. For example, the different body parts of a tiger and of a domestic cat are closely homologous because the two species are very similar genetically. The same kinds of bones and tissues in the same configurations are present in both species. The body parts of the tiger are of course larger; but they are not all simply increased in the same proportion. Instead, natural selection has resulted in each part being increased to a different extent, as required by engineering principles, in order to generate a stable larger structure.

The Schrödinger Paradox

Writing in 1940, Erwin Schrödinger, the inventor of quantum mechanics, inadvertently cast down (or, if you prefer, threw up) a formidable challenge to the purely mechanistic view of life.[5] His book *What Is Life?* posed this insightful question: how can the chemical replication of the genes occur with such a high degree of fidelity, when chemical theory anticipates that a significant frequency of errors must naturally occur in any chemical process? (Schrödinger posed his question even before DNA was recognized as the chemical substance that must be faithfully reproduced.) This question suggests that in the stepwise replication of the DNA of a single gene, one would expect a sufficient number of random errors in the attachment of the appropriate A, T, G, or C unit to the growing chain that would make completely faithful replication impossible. Altered genes would arise on every round of replication. Molecular biologists did not pay much attention to this disconcerting paradox; but some years later, an answer to it was discovered, without reference to Schrödinger's question.

The remarkable answer is *DNA repair.* The theoretically expected occasional mistakes in the chemical process of replication of DNA do indeed occur, but they turn out to be immediately recognized and corrected by a separate, second chemical process that thereby greatly reduces the overall error frequency to acceptably low levels. Such DNA repair already happens in the simplest forms of life we know, the bacteria. To be perfectly explicit, DNA repair is not just a nice trick. Without DNA repair, there could be no stability of species, because DNA replication would be prone to too many natural errors. Life as we know it could not exist. Clearly, this is a particularly graphic example of the necessity for life's basic mechanisms—in this instance, the chemical process of reproduction—to accommodate to the limitations and requirements imposed by the laws of physics and chemistry.

An exceedingly interesting and medically important corollary to this matter of error frequency in chemical replication concerns those viruses (such as HIV and influenza) whose genetic material is RNA rather than DNA. The proliferation of such viruses requires the chemical replication of the viral RNA inside infected cells, a process for which there is no repair mechanism as there is for DNA. RNA replication therefore involves a significant uncorrected error frequency, about one in every 10,000 bases, and such mistakes usually produce mutations in the viral RNA genes. Consequently the proliferation of numerous mutant variants of the virus occurs continually during an infection, and it is therefore difficult for the human immune system to eliminate the virus completely. This accounts in part for the lack of success of antibody-based therapies with HIV and influenza infections.

The Brain and Consciousness

The unknown in biology has always been fertile ground for Vitalistic notions. As one after another of biology's mysteries has been explained entirely by mechanisms that involved physical and chemical operations exclusively, Vitalism has retreated to biological strongholds that are still impenetrable and obscure. The detailed mechanisms of the brain's operations—in particular, the nature of thought and consciousness—are the most pressing of the remaining unknowns of biology. As such, they are also the principal remaining bulwarks of Vitalism. While the molecular and cellular mechanisms involved in various brain functions are yielding to current investigations, the integrated operations of the brain, and especially the nature of thought and consciousness and their relation to brain activity, are still unknown territory. This is not too surprising, since the human brain, with its extremely intricate interaction networks (see Chapter 8), is easily the most complex of living structures.

The extended experience of modern biology encourages the belief that these remaining mysteries will also ultimately have a physical and chemical explanation. But patience is required. After all, until the completely new phenomenon of electricity was discovered around 1800, we had no way of understanding how the mind instructed the body to action or what mechanisms were used to transmit signals in the nervous system. Descartes in 1637 was therefore in the same uncomprehending position about the mind-body problem as we are today about the nature of thought. We must appreciate that many of today's most basic scientific precepts and phenomena were not even guessed at before about 1850: electrical "fields," electromagnetic radiation, atomic structure, quantum mechanics, relativity, nuclear energy, the expanding universe. How can we be certain that there will be no more such key precepts to come? A new kind of energy field associated with the brain seems to be required to understand the generation and the physical nature of thought and consciousness; if this is true, we cannot predict at this time what it will look like and how and when it will be discovered.

Philosophers and others have imputed thought and consciousness to the "mind," implying that mind is more than, and different from, the operations of the brain. Taken literally, this is a form of Vitalism, and it makes no sense to me. The concept of mind as it is applied to thought and consciousness is a nebulous construct, like that of the "soul" as applied to human existence (see pp. 81–82). Like the concept of the soul, the notion of mind may serve a figurative and literary function, but it is a barren substitute for true understanding. Along with others who think about mechanism in biology, for me the mind has no reality apart from the operations of the brain.

For modern humans, thought and consciousness are expressed by a complex language, and they are often considered inseparable from that language. Therefore, since language is a unique and astounding human attribute, some believe that thought and consciousness must also be. But higher animals lacking a complex language can also think, if with much less subtlety than humans. When a deer sees a stalking lion, the deer may not be able to put its reaction into words, but it is certainly equivalent to "I think, therefore I scram." (Whether a deer is also *conscious* of thinking is not clear.) So we must consider thought at least to be independent of, and evolutionarily antecedent to, language acquisition. (Refer also to note 5, Chapter 6.) Beyond that, the mechanisms of thought and consciousness are at present baffling mysteries. Important experimental research is currently being done on the detailed structural and functional correlates of consciousness (that is, what physical and chemical changes are detected and where they occur in the brain when consciousness is stimulated). Such studies will illuminate the phenomena associated with consciousness, but this is not the same as understanding the nature of consciousness itself. Because of this ignorance about the operations of the brain, we are still largely in the dark, unfortunately, with respect to understanding the nature of our internal mental world, which must therefore continue to be considered as autonomous (see Chapter 10).

. . .

In summarizing the main ideas of this chapter, the following points are most important. The axiomatic basis of modern biology is that the activities of life are entirely a matter of chemistry and physics. As astonishingly complex as life is, there is no need to invoke some divine or transcendental intervention to account for it. I demonstrated this axiom by a brief (and, of necessity, oversimplified) overview of modern molecular biology and the knowledge that has been acquired in the latter half of this century about the giant molecules, especially the proteins, RNA, and DNA, which are characteristic of life on Earth. With this knowledge, modern molecular and cellular explanations of some of the many remarkable operations of life have been developed. To demonstrate how chemistry and physics alone can explain how living systems work, I attempted in this chapter to briefly analyze the evolution of life (by way of the processes of gene mutation and natural selection); the reproduction of life (by asexual and, particularly, by sexual mechanisms, the latter attuned to generating genetic diversity within a species as well as generating new species); and the astonishing processes of growth and differentiation of a complex organism from a single fertilized egg cell. Finally, I analyzed some of the arguments used by Vitalists to support their contention that life, especially human life, somehow transcends the laws of physics and chemistry, and I responded to their arguments by relying on modern biological knowledge.

There is a famous story of the occasion when the great French mathematical physicist the Marquis de Laplace encountered Napoleon at a grand ball and explained to him his recent theory of the mechanical origins and structure of the universe. When he finished, Napoleon paused and then asked, "And what role does

God play in your theory?" Laplace replied, "I have no need for that hypothesis." Exactly the same response can be given to Vitalists who insist that the axiomatic basis of modern biology is inadequate to explain life and that a central role for God in the origins and operations of human life in particular is a certainty.

CHAPTER 5

Biological Repair and the Realities of Human Life, Aging, and Death

From time immemorial, humans have been obsessed with death. Death as the terrifying unknown, as the ultimate disaster, has made humans recoil from it: as La Rochefoucauld wrote, "Neither the sun nor death can be looked at steadily." Traditional religions have been invented in part to deny the finality of earthly death, to humble death by confronting it with human immortality in an afterlife. Judeo-Christianity apparently regards death as a mistake: Eve should have refused the fork-tongued offer of fruit from the Tree of Knowledge, or else she should have insisted on the fruit from the Tree of Life. In either case, had she made a better choice, we would now all be immortal and would not have to wait for Eve's terrible mistake to be finally rectified on Judgment Day.

Current medical fantasy even hints that we will not have to wait for Judgment Day to attain immortal life. Why might we not be able to enjoy it on Earth? The great successes of modern medicine have created for many the mirage that human longevity can perhaps be increased indefinitely, that maybe there is even a gene that can be manipulated to turn off death. As Lewis Thomas wrote, "Dying [seems increasingly to be] regarded as the ultimate failure, something that could always be avoided or averted if only the health-care system functioned more efficiently."[1] The science of biology, however, serves as a reality check on these irrationalities, as I demonstrate in this chapter.

It must first be appreciated that the individual life is intrinsically extraordinarily fragile. While to all outward appearances the adult human body appears to be a relatively stable structure over periods of years, researchers began to discover, starting in 1945, that the living organism is in fact a seething cauldron of continual and rapid destruction of molecules and cells and their perpetual regeneration, creating the external impression of a relatively steady overall physical state. These processes of breakdown and repair exist in all living things down to the bacteria and thus appear to be a condition for the stability of life. As such, repair has a profound significance for understanding the mechanical basis of life and death, as we now explore.

In 1945, Rudolf Schönheimer, using the newly available stable nitrogen isotope N^{15} as a tracer, showed that most protein molecules in the body were "turned over"—that is, destroyed, and new ones generated—in a matter of hours or days. Outside the body, though, in a sterile solution in a test tube, a protein molecule can remain unchanged for months at a time. Why the rapid protein turnover in the body? The answer in part is that in the body and inside most cells, many kinds of protein molecules are subject to unavoidable chemical attacks that render them dysfunctional, attacks from poisons like hydrogen peroxide that arise during normal metabolism, from free radicals, from radiation, and so forth. In other words, the operations of chemistry and physics inside the body inescapably wreck protein molecules in time. These chemical defects in protein molecules cannot be reversed. Rather than allowing these defective molecules to clog up the cell's operations, other proteins recognize these defectives and rapidly break them down to reusable pieces (amino acids). New protein molecules are then made in cells to replace the ones destroyed, so as to maintain the amount of a functional protein fairly constant.

Most cells in the body also turn over. The average red blood cell, for example, has a half life of about 100 days in the human body, until it is inevitably destroyed by, among other traumas, the continual physical wear it receives from being squeezed through the capillaries numerous times. Mechanisms that program cell death exist in the simplest single cell as well as in the most complex organisms. Presumably these mechanisms detect a cell that has undergone some initial chemical events that would ultimately and inevitably result in cell death and then proceed to accelerate the cell killing process. The cells that die are replaced by new ones. (Nerve cells of the brain by contrast, however, have long lives; and when they finally die, new ones are not normally regenerated in humans.)

All of this destruction and regeneration of molecules and cells is tremendously costly to the organism, requiring the commitment of huge amounts of energy to repair processes. (Imagine if everyone had to bring their automobiles into the shop to have the engine, transmission, fuel system, brakes—the whole works—repaired every hour of every day!) It is clear that this turnover is essential to life; namely, that it is an elaborate response that allows the organism to survive the rigors of the chemical and physical environments inside living cells and the body. As these facts indicate, life is so organized as to persist in the face of inescapable chemical and physical assaults—still another example of how life must conform to the constraints imposed by physics and chemistry. Repair must and does occur at all levels of living systems. Most protein molecules turn over in a matter of hours or days, cells turn over in a matter of months or years, and whole organisms turn over (that is, they die and new ones are born) in a matter of many decades. Deaths of old individuals and births of new ones constitute the species' mechanism for its persistence over hundreds of millennia. That is what reproduction is all about; it is to compensate for inevitable death. That is why the capacity to reproduce is one of the key definitions of the living state. Immortality would not require reproduction. At the highest level, entire species may become extinct and new ones arise as part of evolution's mechanisms to ensure that life itself is maintained.

Now let's defy tradition and look at death steadily for a while. The death of an individual can be caused by any one of a large number of factors, some arising from the external environment, others from internal malfunctions of the organism. (John Webster was probably on the right track when he wrote: "...death hath its ten thousand several doors / For man to make his exit.") Some of the major external factors have been predation (mainly in wars with other people), starvation and famines, natural catastrophes, and bacterial, viral, and other infectious agents. Of internal factors that can bring about death, one class results from the eventual breakdown of one or more of the multitude of repair processes within the body that were just discussed. Another class of internal factors involves a variety of aberrant processes that are unfortunately not normally reparable. Between them, these two classes of internal factors are responsible for one or another of a wide range of fatal diseases, such as atherosclerosis and heart disease, stroke, muscular dysfunction, Alzheimer's disease and other neuro-degenerative diseases, all the many kinds of cancer, kidney failure, failure of the immune system, liver degeneration, diabetes, and many more. Each such killer disease ultimately results from the deleterious action of a specific single protein of the body or of a particular set of proteins, and hence involves the specific genes that encode these proteins.

The evolution of life has had a great stake in regulating death.[2] This is because the persistence of a species over time obviously requires that the number of individuals who die in a given time interval must not regularly exceed the number who survive. If, instead, the number who die is significantly and persistently smaller than the number of survivors, the population of that species will increase indefinitely, and the essential long-term balance among all species that is a hallmark of evolution (see Chapter 7) will be destroyed. So evolution has walked a tightrope. In order to maintain the balance among species, natural selection, operating through the genes involved, has seen to it that the average life span of the individuals of each surviving species is maintained within fairly narrow bounds, not too short to result in extinction, but not too long to produce overpopulation.

Thus, the average longevity of human beings has not been simply a randomly determined number. Until recent centuries, it has been the result of many hundreds of thousands of years of slow-acting evolutionary adaptation of the species to the many external and internal factors that can be the cause of death.[3] For most of the past several million years of human existence, the food supply was probably severely limiting, and starvation was the most powerful brake on the size of human population. In that situation, in order for the species to survive, the various internal factors capable of causing death had to be suppressed during evolution, staved off until a late stage of life. This was accomplished by natural selection of, on the one hand, genes that maintained intact the great multitude of internal repair processes into later life and, on the other hand, genes that postponed those aberrant and irreparable processes capable of causing death.

What evidence exists suggests that the resultant average life span of early humans was about 20 years. (This average included, at the low end of the age spectrum, many deaths at birth or shortly afterward and, at the high end, a few at the ages of 80 to 90 years.) This average life span ensured the survival of the species but allowed only a relatively slow increase over time in the human population. Only 10,000 years ago, however, this situation was entirely unsettled by the invention of agriculture (as discussed in Chapter 7). A more ample food supply considerably reduced deaths by starvation. The ensuing 10,000 years have been insufficient time for natural selection to compensate for this reduction in death by starvation. The average life span has accordingly increased, and the human population entered an explosive exponential expansion that has continued to the present day. Even so, a little over 100 years ago, Americans had an average life span of 40 years, or only about twice that of early humans millions of years ago. Today, just a century later, our average life span is close to 80 years. This stunningly rapid increase has been widely viewed with enthusiasm, yet it has the little appreciated potential for inflicting enormous damage on our society and its economy.[4] But this dismal socioeconomic prospect, as obviously critical as it is, at this point is not the focus of our attention, which is primarily biological. How did this very large and rapid change in average life span occur? Does it mean that the average life span can be manipulated to increase indefinitely?

In only the past 100 years or so, what has happened is that beyond a more ample food supply, many of the other external factors capable of causing death have been either drastically suppressed or eliminated in Western societies by various measures, among those affluent enough to afford them, including improved sanitation, a better diet, the introduction of antibiotics to control deadly bacterial infections, and immunizations against bacterial, viral, and other diseases. This rapid melioration of many important external factors causing death has not given natural selection the time to compensate by selecting for different alleles of the genes that control the internal factors. Americans and other Westerners are therefore now dying increasingly later in life from the unaltered internal factors that in previous millennia did not add substantially to the large number of deaths produced by then-prevalent external factors. Hence the many diseases determined by internal factors, such as heart disease, cancer, and others listed earlier, have become the major causes of death.

As one strange consequence of these circumstances, some of today's most important fatal diseases were not even recognized as recently as a century ago. Take Alzheimer's disease, for example. It was first described by Alois Alzheimer in 1906, when it was very rare. Today, it is a major cause of death: by the age of 90, one of every two humans is likely to be affected by it. Alzheimer's disease seems to be one of those I previously classified as produced by internal processes that are aberrant and not reparable. In the human population, the genes involved in this aberrant process have apparently been selected during evolution to produce a toxic agent that accumulates only slowly and that on average does not begin to produce fatal results until after 65 years of age. In other words, early human evolution selected for the suppression of Alzheimer's disease until a then-rare old age; but because of the recent extension of the average life span to 80 years, Alzheimer's disease has now gone from being unknown to being a major scourge. Similarly, many other fatal diseases caused by internal factors have today become prominent for the first time.

What does all this mean for the prospects of further and possibly unlimited increases in human longevity? It is clear that between 75 and 100 years of age humans today become increasingly susceptible to a very large range of those fatal diseases caused by various internal factors. As these problems swiftly descend one after another upon an aging individual, their amelioration by medical intervention is often extremely costly—and as each problem is individually dealt with, the next is likely to be on its way. Furthermore, apart from this multitude of potentially fatal diseases, a great army of misery-inducing conditions is mobilized against the aging person: arthritis, pain, brittle bones, enlarged prostates, incontinence, pain, failing hearing and vision, loss of sexual potency, pain, erosion of memory, depression, helplessness, thankless children, and so on. As one experienced wag has put it, as one ages, everything either dries up or starts to leak. Thus, while only limited extensions of aged life can be anticipated from medical advances, they will inevitably be accompanied by an increasing deterioration in the quality of life for most of the elderly. The conclusion is brilliantly clear: under present circumstances, the average life span *cannot* be extended indefinitely in a personally tolerable way.

The only biological escape from this conclusion is the remote possibility that some unknown master gene could be manipulated to turn off, or at least greatly postpone, most of these numerous fatal or misery-producing conditions more or less simultaneously. But the existence of such a single master gene, one that could control so many different biological processes, seems unlikely to me. Furthermore, even if such a master gene existed, and we could learn how to modify it suitably, how could such a gene transformation be widely disseminated in the human population? Or would it be the exclusive privilege of those who could pay for it?

Besides these biological reality checks on the mirage of the indefinite extension of human life, serious difficulties in providing health care for the aged loom on the horizon for society as a whole. If current trends persist, the resulting economic encumbrances for our society will become very burdensome.[5] Health care expenditures for the elderly have outpaced the gross domestic product (GDP) by 3.5 to 4.0 percent per year in recent decades. This increase is the consequence of two changes: the rapid increase in the proportion of the elderly in the population, and the continuous escalation of the cost of medical technology that is used to postpone death. In 1900, only 4 percent of the U.S. population was over 65 years of age. Today that figure is 13 percent, and by 2030 it is projected to be over 20 percent. (This increase is despite the effects of immigration, which increases the younger age groups.) In addition, medical technology has become ever more complex and expensive over time. If the present course continues unabated, these factors suggest that health care consumption by the elderly may cost more than $30,000 per year per person by 2020 (in 1995 dollars, when the cost was $9,200). With the current distribution of health care payments between the public and private sectors, these projected costs in 2020 will require an enormous increase in taxes as well as a substantial decrease in the living standards of the elderly. These and other socioeconomic problems will only be exacerbated by further increases in the average life span.

The present "me first" approach of the majority of Americans to problems of health care is largely egocentric, with no awareness of the societal perspective. In that climate, it is understandable that the average 80-year-old expects society to pay for expensive kidney dialysis to treat kidney failure, or to provide access to expensive open-heart surgery if the individual is afflicted with a heart attack or atherosclerosis, or to pay for a hip replacement if it would improve mobility—all with no questions asked. Medical intervention to prolong life is considered a right of the elderly, irrespective of the low additional life expectancy or of the cumulative effects of such costs on the society. Unfortunately, this is not a tenable long-term policy.

Underlying and basic to all these critical concerns are the largely uninformed and naïve views of the nature of aging and death that are held by the irrational majority as well as the complacence of physicians and medical researchers toward these problems. Rationalists urgently need to work toward the acceptance of sane and reality-based views of aging and death. Scientific research and medical technology that are directed to expanding human longevity *per se* should be viewed with a serious concern that the biological as well as the social realities of the human condition are being disregarded.*

Death is the ultimate and unavoidable result of the degradative operations of physics, chemistry, and biology acting on the body's molecules, cells, and organs.

---

* The ancient wisdom offered by the myth of Eos and Tithonus has compelling relevance to the irresistible human impulse to prolong one's life no matter what. Tithonus was a prince of Troy with whom Eos, the goddess of the dawn, became enamored. When she took him as her spouse, he begged her to grant him immortality such as she possessed, and she cajoled Zeus into doing so. But in asking

Death is thus not a curse visited upon humanity because of its ancestral transgressions. Death is instead an integral part of life. It is not an independent event inflicted on the living, one that can somehow be circumvented by advanced medical technology. Immortality is not biologically, let alone socially, feasible. Death, though, resists rational and dispassionate analysis. Its effects are too devastating. The loss of a loved one is one of the cruelest blows that life can inflict; for some, it makes their own lives no longer meaningful or endurable. Our primitive impulses have been not only to deny death as long as possible but also to invest the aftermath of death with Vitalistic ideas and practices that have always had great appeal and enormous power. The existence of an immortal soul independent of the body; the transmigration of a soul after death into another human or animal body; the coming of a Judgment Day when immortal souls will all be either elevated to Heaven to join God forever more or thrust into Hell to be eternally consumed by the fires of Satan—these are some of the fabulous notions that human beings have invented and that many deeply believe in today. Burial instead of cremation of our dead is an atavistic sacramental practice that is grounded in such special fantasies. Yet the axiomatic basis of modern biology can afford these Vitalistic ideas no credibility. They are myths. A

---

for his eternal life, she failed to ask for his eternal youth. The grievous result was the subject of Tennyson's great and despairing poem "Tithonus":

> The woods decay, the woods decay and fall,
> The vapors weep their burthen to the ground,
> Man comes and tills the field and lies beneath,
> And after many a summer dies the swan.
> Me only cruel immortality
> Consumes; I wither slowly in thine arms...

"soul" existing and operating apart from the body is a magical notion, but it has no physical meaning. (What would power its many
independent functions? Soular energy? How is memory retained
by the soul without an attached living brain, which is the seat of
all memory?) Death is simply the end of the living state; the "I
myself" vanishes, never to return. The dead organism, no longer
able to consume and transform the energy required to maintain
life, becomes an inanimate mass, to be decomposed by bacteria,
insects, and worms into the molecules that will go to produce new
life. This is simplicity itself, but it is understandably not an attractive prospect for many human beings, who fervently want to
believe in an individual immortality, if not on Earth, then in an
afterlife, which many religions promise them and their loved
ones.* For rationalists, however, the exercise of reason about the
nature of life and death cannot be shunted aside by fantasy.

---

* The technology of cloning human beings, by the way, if it is ever condoned,
could produce a newborn that is *genetically* identical to the individual whose DNA
was used. But when the newborn becomes an adult, the clone would be *culturally*
entirely different, with no retention of the memory or experience of its clonal antecedent. Such a *tabula rasa* clone would therefore be a new person, and not really an instrument of individual immortality.

CHAPTER 6

Behavior and the Genes

If man is indeed the proper study of mankind, as Pope asserted, then it is human behavior that warrants the closest scrutiny if we wish to understand the affairs of the world. In the past, human behavior has largely been the province of psychology, anthropology, and the literary imagination to explore. But a new age has dawned. In the modern era, thinking people have begun to appreciate that biological science has much to contribute to our understanding of human character. That contribution is the important subject of this chapter.

First, a definition. A behavior can be defined as any mentally directed activity by which an animal organism interacts with its environment, including its responses to stimuli from the environment. The general term *behavior* refers to the sum total of these activities. In everyday language, human behavior is based

on such deep-seated characteristics as intelligence, aggression, altruism, sexuality, greed, spirituality, sensitivity, and so on. These
characteristics direct the values and specific behavioral responses
that each individual brings to the world. But human behavior is
labyrinthine, extraordinarily complicated. At this early stage in
our perception of behavior, we can only hope to make out some
of its boundaries.

The question of what determines basic human characteristics
and behavior has intrigued thinkers throughout recorded history.
Two sets of elements have long been discriminated as influential,
one set that is fixed or innate for any one individual, and another
that is malleable or learned, the latter based on what information and attitudes the individual absorbs from the environment.
Common-sense experience led the ancients to recognize the existence of fixed elements of human behavior, which they attributed to a person's fate or destiny or to the influence of the stars.
Oedipus could not escape his fate, and so his overweening pride
led him unknowingly to kill his father in a fit of rage. And as Kent
avows when he reflects on the character differences between
Cordelia and Lear's other two daughters,

> It is the stars
> The stars above us, govern our conditions;
> Else one self mate and mate could not beget
> Such different issues.

Modern biology, however, has shown us that the fixed elements of
our behavior are programmed by our genes, not our stars. Our
genes in considerable part direct our fate. Siblings born of the same
parents, as we have seen, while genetically related to one another,
are perforce genetically different. That Cordelia's behavior is dif-

ferent, even very different, from that of her sisters, despite their common upbringing, is therefore not inexplicable genetically.

In the modern world, the key issue in our understanding of adult human behavior is, then, what are the relative roles of the genes and of the environment in its determination? This is the old conundrum, nature versus nurture, brought up to date. In order to explore this issue from a biological point of view, we must first realize that biologists do not segregate humans conceptually from the rest of the animal kingdom, as do many nonbiologists. Evolution has deep functional as well as taxonomic significance for biologists. They are aware that patterns of behavior, quite often highly complex, are found throughout the animal kingdom, not just among humans. In evolutionarily earlier life forms, as with the insects and birds, these remarkable behaviors are almost entirely innate, not acquired by learning. They include, for example, the incredible organization and activities of insect societies and the amazing fidelity of annual bird migrations. These behaviors must somehow be encoded in the genes, although which and how many genes and gene-encoded products participate in any one instance are still mostly unknown. As species evolved, however, natural selection apparently favored the appearance of those with larger and more intricate nervous systems and brains, which allowed greater reliance on mechanisms for the learning of behavior and proportionately less dependence on fixed genetic programs. Modern humans, with their extraordinary brains, are the species in which this balance between fixed and learned behavior has been most extensively shifted toward the learning mode.

Many people in our society seem to believe that for humans this shift is all but complete: that each of us starts out as a *tabula rasa*, a clean slate, and that all behavior is subsequently learned, with no or only a minor role for the genes. I know of no previous culture in history in which fixed or innate elements of human behavior have been so thoroughly denigrated.[1] This view is to my mind regressive. It is the legacy of the eighteenth-century Enlightenment, many of whose eminent figures believed in the perfectibility of the human being through appropriate education and experience. Modern so-called behaviorists have inherited much of this tradition. Later in this chapter, however, I will present some of the evidence and arguments that support the contrary view, namely, that basic kinds of human behavior are to a very significant extent fixed, as programmed in the genes.

At this point, however, I want to set one seeming paradox straight. It is obviously true that humans learn essentially all their behaviors from birth to maturity from their environment. Learning and experience are uniquely individual, and they help to make each person singular. But that does *not* signify that the genes do not participate in the processes of learning and experiencing. The evidence supports the view that each individual's genetic makeup greatly influences, from the cradle to adulthood, his or her capacities for the learning of behavior. To account for the evidence from behavioral studies of identical twins, as described later on, one must conclude that the genes largely determine what an individual is *able* to learn, what one selects from experience to retain or emphasize, and how one transforms such selective learning into basic kinds of behavior. Furthermore, recalling the genetic diversity that is inherent in the human species, this view therefore means that each individual brings a different genetic background to bear on what one learns, what one comes to believe, and how one learns to behave. In this scenario, the essential roles of the environment and of learning are not so much to determine an individual's basic behavior, but rather to influence the extent to which the more or less fixed genetic potential of that basic behavior is realized and specifically directed. In this view, there was no way that Ronald Reagan, however his early environment might have been rearranged, could have become another Albert Einstein; on the other hand, without proper infant nutrition, a decent family life, and a good education, all acquired by nurture, it is highly probable that Albert Einstein would not have fully achieved his own genetic potential.[2]

Such views are not widely palatable in the public domain these days, partly because they have often been misrepresented for political purposes—for example, by Social Darwinism, which, without warrant, co-opts the notion of the survival of the fittest from the biological into the social domain. Before I explore the evidence to support these views, it might first be helpful to my non-biologist readers to review some of the innate behaviors of evolutionarily earlier forms of life, in order to appreciate the immense power of the genes in determining very intricate behavior. The power of the genes in specifying behavior is extraordinary. Once such a genetic capability arises by natural selection, it may be ramified or redirected, but it is not wholly lost. It is reasonable to infer that such genetic power must have been transmitted in various ways during evolution to human beings. Of the many possible examples, I have selected two spectacular instances of the genetic control of behavior to present in some detail.

The first involves the cuckoo bird. The adult female cuckoo usually lays her egg in the nest of another species of bird, who then unknowingly broods the cuckoo egg along with her own. (This habit already has its counterpart in human behavior. Jean-

Jacques Rousseau, to take one example, that eminent humanitarian and enthusiast for the proper education of children, fathered five offspring, all of whom he gave up to be raised in foster homes or orphanages.) Different cuckoo species have eggs of different colors and sizes, and each species deposits its egg only in the nest of a host bird whose eggs look similar to that particular cuckoo's. But the best part of cuckoo behavior is yet to come. The newly hatched cuckoo in its foster nest, only two days old—and *before its eyes are opened*—will push out of the nest any and all other still unhatched eggs of the resident mother bird that it encounters. This behavior, having great survival value, enables the fledgling cuckoo to thrive under the keener attention of the foster mother. Such behavior is obviously innate; the newborn cuckoo has had no time to learn it. As to its nature, this behavior should be entirely familiar to anyone in our society: it is similar to what one might expect from a fledgling version of a John D. Rockefeller or a Bill Gates, elbowing some fellow preschooler away from the ice cream supply. But it is all programmed in the genes of the cuckoo. (Might it also be in its human analog?) Nor is this the whole story. The newborn cuckoo must convince its foster mother to feed it. To do so, it innately produces a begging signal that so well mimics that of the parent birds' true offspring (say, a warbler) that the parents are deceived into providing the single cuckoo with the food that would have otherwise gone to as many as four warbler chicks.[3] This deception works, even though, within a few days after hatching, the fledging cuckoo is already twice as large as the warbler parent.

As a second example of the genetic control of a complex behavior, consider the construction of spider webs. Many of us have no doubt been fascinated at one time or another watching a spider build a gorgeous web. Those species of spiders that spin webs rely on them completely for their food supply, so these webs are not just a casual artistic display; they have been refined during evolution by the processes of natural selection to enable these spider species to survive. The spinning of webs is not learned. If spiders are raised from birth in isolation from other spiders and are then released into the wild on reaching maturity, they proceed immediately to construct that species' characteristic webs. The first web is already perfect. The information for web spinning is therefore innate in these spiders. It must somehow be encoded in their genes. This genetic program includes the structural features of web spinning, such as the extraordinary properties of the several kinds of spider silk proteins that make them so suitable for producing ultra-thin threads of great tensile strength and appropriate elasticity and the special body parts (the silk glands and the spinnerets) involved in the spinning process. But I am not here concerned so much with the material components of web spinning, remarkable as they are, as I am with the spinning operations themselves. These operations in their most highly evolved forms constitute an astonishing feat of engineering know-how, but no spider ever had to go to MIT to learn how to do it. (For those interested, some of the almost incredible details are collected in several sources listed in my notes.[4])

From observing many of the operations of web spinning, one gets the eerie impression of a superior engineering intelligence at work. Spinning an orb web, for example, is not simply a stereotyped affair repeated in identical fashion each time. The spider must apparently make several decisions and choices during its travails. The first critical choice is to locate the web in a place that minimizes the chance of its destruction by wind or animal movements and maximizes the efficiency of capture of the appropriate sizes and kinds of flying insects in the vicinity. Another choice is that of appropriate anchoring sites on a tree branch, a roof or porch, a fence, or whatever for the three-point web framework that best orients the planar orb web for the capture of flying prey and ensures its structural stability. Yet another choice is how to perform the particular sequence of laying down the radial threads within the framework so as to maintain the web's stability throughout its construction. Then comes the subsequent decision about when to switch spinning from one kind of silk gland to another that contains the more sticky thread of the spiral web itself. These are only some of the choices made each time a web is spun. As a result, no two orb webs made by a particular spider are identical, although each clearly follows the same basic design.

After the web is constructed, the spider then displays a complex set of behaviors connected with the rapid capture of the prey that lands on its web, which also involve nonstereotyped but programmed responses. Finally, if the web is damaged, the spider has to decide whether it is reparable—and then proceed to carry out repairs appropriate for the particular damage—or whether it is better to start over with a new web. Since each instance of web damage is different, the spider's response is suited to the particular repair required. That is, the response is not stereotyped but shows decision making by the spider. This exercise of choice ("free will"?), however, appears to be entirely a result of the influence and actions of the genes. Realize how remarkable this is. Even those of us who are ready to accept a role for the genes in behavior probably would expect that role to be confined to a highly stereotyped behavior, as performed, say, by an army of marching ants. The spider's web-spinning behavior, on the other hand, shows that the genes also have the capacity to program for, and to elicit, decision making and choice.

I go into this in detail because I am enormously impressed by this expression of what, if performed by humans, would be considered highly intelligent behavior,[5] of a kind that requires learning and experience to perfect. But for solitary spiders, this intelligent behavior appears to be determined by the genes. The specific genes that participate and how their encoded proteins collectively function to elicit this spectacular behavior are entirely unknown. (Spiders have about 20,000 protein-encoding genes, compared to the 50,000 to 100,000 possessed by humans.)

I can imagine some behaviorist psychologists or other social scientists contemplating the two examples described here. Perhaps they would be intrigued and disturbed by them, but because they have had little direct experience with genes and genetic mechanisms, they might shrug them off as having only minor relevance to human behavior. I think this would be a gross mistake. Although we do not yet know exactly how the genes and their protein products exert their complex behavioral influences at the molecular and cellular levels, their power to do so is clear. Evolution, having selected for such power, would very probably have maintained and transmitted the genetic mechanisms involved from earlier life forms to later ones. It is helpful to keep this in mind as I proceed to examine the evidence for a strong genetic influence on basic human behavior. This evidence is powerful but mostly indirect, partly because genetic experiments cannot be carried out directly upon humans, but mainly because present-day biological science cannot yet cope with behavioral phenomena that call into play the combined influence of large numbers, perhaps hundreds, of genes.

First, let's look briefly into current thinking about the nature and acquisition of spoken language. Speaking a language is a form of human behavior. Common sense seems to suggest that language acquisition is the quintessential example of a behavior that is entirely attributable to nurture, to environmental influences. A child must learn a language from the cradle on and acquires language skills progressively from social contacts as he or she matures. Furthermore, given the enormous diversity of specific languages expressed in the world, a common genetic basis for language seems implausible.

Nevertheless, a revolution started 50 years ago by Noam Chomsky has led to the widely accepted view that there is indeed a profound genetic basis for language acquisition in humans. (Many of the psychologists who advocate this view have difficulty, possibly genetic in origin, articulating the words "gene" or "genetic" and so usually refer to the "innate" capacity for language acquisition or to the language "instinct," but genetic influences are what they are talking about.) Although the details of these arguments are complex,[6] the manifesto of the Chomskian revolution is essentially that the human brain—structured by the actions of the genes via their protein products—somehow encodes for a "universal grammar" that is intrinsic to *all* human languages, however much specific languages may differ. These genes, in the absence of any abnormal perturbations, apparently program for the construction of a neural network in the brain into which the elements of specific languages are expeditiously incorporated by each of us. But the nature of these genes and their diversity in the population, as well as the properties and functions of the putative network in the brain, are entirely unknown at present. Although little direct evidence exists, it nevertheless seems highly likely that humans have a capacity for a universal grammar that is programmed in their genes. Given the allelic diversity that characterizes most genes, it seems probable that some part of the differences in the language skills of different individuals might result from this genetic diversity.

Language acquisition may serve as a useful paradigm for other kinds of human behaviors. I explore this stimulating possibility later on, after considering other indirect evidence supporting a crucial role for the genes in influencing a broad range of human behaviors.

Particularly informative have been behavioral studies carried out on human twins. Twins are of two kinds, fraternal and identical. The former arise from an infrequent event: two independently fertilized eggs are nearly simultaneously implanted in a woman's uterus and produce two separate embryos that come to term at the same time. Fraternal twins are thus genetically different, equivalent to any other two siblings born at different times to the same mother and father. Consequently, fraternal twins can be of different sexes and may look no more alike than any other two siblings. Identical twins, in contrast, arise from a single fertilized egg when, on relatively rare occasions in early embryonic development, the single embryo splits into two and each embryonic fragment goes on to develop fully. (If this process occurs too late in embryonic development and is incomplete, Siamese twins result.) As a consequence, identical twins have identical genetic endowments, which are, of course, reflected in their same sex and nearly indistinguishable physical features.

Identical twins therefore permit a kind of natural experiment: namely, one can observe and compare the basic behavioral characteristics of two humans whose genetic constitution is identical but who, if they were reared apart from a very early age, have been subjected to different sets of environmental influences. The basic behavioral characteristics of identical twins reared apart, presumably under significantly different conditions, can be compared with those behaviors of other identical twins reared together, presumably under closely similar conditions. If the environment is the primary influence on behavior, then the behaviors of any two identical twins reared apart should on average be quite significantly different; with twins reared together, the behaviors should be much more similar. By contrast, if genes are the primary influence, then identical twins reared apart should show strongly correlated behaviors that are not significantly different from the correlated behaviors of other such twins reared together. This enables us to explore the relative behavioral influence of genes and of the environment—of nature and nurture.

Careful scientific studies along these lines have been carried out, particularly by the Minnesota Center for Twin and Adoption Research, which was established in 1979. T. J. Bouchard and his colleagues summarized much of this excellent work in 1988 and 1990. (For references to these original publications, consult Appendix F, which also includes two summary tables.) Because quantitative measures of behavior, such as IQ tests for intelligence, are controversial, the investigators generally used several accepted tests for each behavior measured. What is more, even if the absolute value of a behavioral measurement such as IQ is controversial, when it is used as a relative measure of behavior between two groups of individuals, as in the twin studies, it has significance.

The results were clear. The average correlation for a behavioral measure between mature identical twins reared apart was generally quite high, ranging between 0.5 and 0.7 for a given behavior. (A correlation value of 1.0 represents a perfect correlation;

0.0 is a complete absence of correlation, such as we observe on average with any two randomly chosen individuals.) For a physical attribute such as fingerprint details, the correlation value was 0.97, close to 1.0, as expected. For IQ, the correlation was 0.7 to 0.8, a quite large value. Even more remarkable, however, the average correlation for almost all basic behaviors measured for mature identical twins reared together was not significantly different from the average correlation for identical twins reared apart. Hence no environmental influence was detectable. In addition to IQ, a wide range of psychological, personality, and other basic behavioral characteristics, such as well-being, social potency, achievement, stress reaction, alienation, aggression, and traditionalism, were measured for the identical twins (see Appendix F, Table 1), with much the same results.

The comparison between identical and fraternal twins reared apart or together (see Appendix F, Table 2) was also revealing. The average correlation coefficients for several behavioral characteristics were about half as large for fraternal twins as for identical ones who were reared either apart or together. Given that two fraternal twins have 50 percent genetic identity, compared to 100 percent for two identical twins, this value of half is consistent with a primary genetic role in determining these behaviors. Reinforcing this inference, fraternal twins reared together showed no greater correlation coefficients for these behaviors than did fraternal twins who had been reared apart; a significant environmental influence on these behaviors was thus not detected.

It should also be appreciated that a number of factors that could conceivably produce behavioral differences between identical twins have nothing to do with learning from the environment; collectively, they might be called epigenetic. These epigenetic effects might result from differences in gene expression in the twins—promoted, for example, by the different embryonic environments of those identical twins (roughly one-third) who mature in independent amniotic sacs in the same uterus—or from certain diseases that might affect the behavior of one developing twin and not the other. Such epigenetic factors might induce variant behavior between identical twins, which would unknowingly serve to decrease the influence that would otherwise be attributed to the genes.[7]

The data indicate a profound and primary influence of the genes on many aspects of adult human personality and behavior. Furthermore, it is surprising to find that the effects on many basic behavioral characteristics of adult twins who had been reared in different environments from an early age are negligible. The conclusion that intelligence, personality, and other basic behavioral differences are influenced more by genetics than by environmental factors is difficult to circumvent. This conclusion has now been supported by many independent worldwide studies. These studies used several different types of behavioral comparisons—not only of identical twins reared together and reared apart but also of fraternal twins, of adoptive parents compared to their offspring, and of adoptive siblings. Yet this conclusion runs counter to popular intuition, to much current thinking in the social sciences, and to the belief systems of many altruistic rationalists, all of which accord to the environment the primary role in molding behavior. (To have anticipated otherwise is something like expecting that Martin Luther would have believed Copernicus and would have become convinced that the Earth rotates around a stationary sun.) But when the clamor is over, rationalists must understand, accept, and cope with the stubborn facts.

A way to grasp this phenomenon is to understand that a primary role for the genes in determining basic human behavior means that human beings are essentially as diverse in their collected behaviors as they are in their physical features—their sizes, physiognomies, hair and eye colors, fingerprints, and so forth. Most of us are readily distinguished from our fellow humans by this collection of genetically determined physical features. For similar reasons, we are most probably also individually distinctive in our basic behavioral characteristics.

As fundamental as what these facts mean, however, is what they do *not* mean. They do *not* mean that the environment is unimportant to human behavior. On the contrary, an appropriately nourishing and supportive environment is absolutely crucial to the full development of each individual human being's genetic potential. Experiments with animals have shown that poor nutrition shortly after birth can result in incomplete development of the maturing brain, which cannot be corrected in later life. Poverty and abuse can lead to stunted development, low self-esteem, and many other barriers to self-fulfillment.

Furthermore, a particular cultural environment can clearly fix many of the *specific* habits and mores of people. Here the example of language acquisition that we considered earlier may be useful. A distinction was made between the many specific languages, on the one hand, and, on the other, a universal grammar that appears to underlie all of them. Whether an individual learns to speak English or Swahili can be thought of as a specific behavior, which is clearly primarily acquired from the environment. But basic to the acquisition of a specific language is a genetically determined capacity for learning a language that is universal to all humans, encoding a *universal*—or what we have earlier called *basic*—behavior. Similarly, we may think of most human behaviors as involving both specific and basic components, the former derived mainly from environmental contributions, the latter from genetic. Which types of clothing people wear; whether they eat with their fingers, or chopsticks, or knives and forks; whether they wipe their noses with a banana leaf or with a Kleenex—these are specific behaviors that are mainly influenced by the environment and not by the genes. But people's interest in covering their bodies to keep warm, their need to propel nourishment into their mouths (starting with breast feeding), or their desire to keep their noses clean so that they can breath freely are basic human behavioral characteristics that are very likely genetically determined.

Certain kinds of human behaviors can be instilled by operant conditioning, in response to receiving rewards or avoiding punishments. Experience has proved that when such environmental conditioning is particularly intensive and has been practiced for generations in a human population—as in the inculcation of religious beliefs, the cultivation of self-interest in capitalist societies, the arousal of xenophobic hatreds by demagogues—the modification of individual and mass behavior has been very effectual. All of this indicates that, without a doubt, the environment can affect at least certain types of behavior. Environmental as well as genetic influences contribute considerably to the tremendous diversity of individual behavioral characteristics.

A strong genetic influence on basic human behavior, including intelligence, has momentous meaning for society. Sexual reproduction in the context of genetic diversity means that fine intelligence, even genius, can sometimes arise in an individual from a particular constellation of genes (see Appendix D) derived at random from two relatively undistinguished parents living in poor social circumstances. History abounds with famous examples. Leonardo da Vinci was the son of an unmarried peasant father and mother; Isaac Newton was born of an illiterate farm couple; and Albert Einstein was the son of a lower-middle-class couple, with a father who was a failed businessman. The environments in which these geniuses were raised cannot possibly account for their uniqueness. Conversely, many brilliant people have produced offspring who were much more ordinary than themselves. These events are to be anticipated occasionally, as discussed earlier, from the genetic diversification that is produced by sexual reproduction.

In a true democracy, as a matter of principle, equal opportunity for every citizen should be an inalienable right, whatever the social circumstances. Biology crucially adds that such equal opportunity is a necessity, because we have no way to assess in advance the genetic potential of any one unique individual. A human being should therefore be treated as an individual, not as a statistic on a bell curve. This is a severe problem in our inner cities, where poverty and lack of opportunity are endemic. It is not enough to ensure the bare survival of the young in these circumstances, because the impotence of unrealized potential that is imposed by the environment is self-perpetuating and usually overwhelming. To create the opportunities of education, decent health services, and constructive recreation for potentially useful young citizens in inner cities, we need to direct to the poor certainly not less, and not just the same, *but even more* than the usual investment in our society's more affluent children.[8] Cost effectiveness is not a criterion for political democracy. And that is the nature of the dilemma. Commitment to a true political democracy would require most of the better-off in our society to turn their value system around by 180 degrees.

A primary genetic influence on basic kinds of behavior cannot be construed to mean that a single gene exists for each kind of behavior. There is unlikely to be a single gene for altruistic behavior or a gene that uniquely influences intelligence. Almost certainly many genes, probably hundreds, contribute to influence each kind of basic behavior. At present, we do not know how scientifically to identify the members of these sets of genes, many of which may overlap. One can expect that some of these genes dictate precise structures that develop during the brain's growth, along with the precise extent to which some of these structures can subsequently be modified by learning; these might simultaneously affect a number of different behaviors. Even if we wanted to, therefore, we cannot now contemplate carrying out genetic engineering of any human behavior, because we do not know which and how many genes to manipulate.

A powerful genetic determination of basic behavior plays havoc with society's current views about the degree to which humans possess free will—and therefore with the extent to which they can be held willfully responsible for their actions. Our legal and justice systems are structured on the proposition of personal responsibility for criminal behavior, with exceptions granted only for acts committed by the insane. From the perspective of protecting members of society from criminal behavior, it may be of little consequence whether a crime is considered to be a purely willful act of malevolence or is conditioned by a brutal environment or is in good part programmed in the criminal's genes: the desire to sequester the criminal from society is independent of the causative mechanism for the crime. But the laws and the administration of justice should eventually be based on scientific knowledge of human behavior. Just as we no longer solve society's problems by burning witches, we ultimately need to understand both the genetic and environmental causes of human criminal behavior and base our criminal laws and prospects of rehabilitation on rationality, without condoning crime. Understanding the basis of criminal behavior does not mean accepting it.

Can it be possible that behavioral genetics also has something important to say about education? (I already hear my colleagues' screams of fury.) If what can be learned by an individual is substantially influenced by that person's genetic makeup, one might indeed expect so. One of our greatest poets and most eminent humanists wrote the following:

> When I heard the learn'd astronomer,
> When the proofs, the figures, were ranged in columns before
>   me,
> When I was shown the charts and diagrams, to add, divide, and
>   measure them,
> When I sitting heard the astronomer where he lectured with
>   much applause in the lecture-room,
> How soon unaccountable I became tired and sick,
> Till rising and gliding out I wandered off by myself,
> In the mystical moist night-air, and from time to time,
> Look'd up in perfect silence at the stars.
> —*Walt Whitman, 1865*

If Whitman could write this, then perhaps that brilliant man did not have an adequate complement of the appropriate alleles of the genes necessary to cope with scientific abstractions. Many of us who are science teachers remember more than a few students who appeared likewise tired and sick—and sometimes the reverse—during our lectures. Well, fine and dandy. Maybe these potential

Whitmans should not be forced to try to cope with the abstract sciences but instead should be allowed to concentrate only on subjects better suited to their genetic predispositions. What they need to know about science and technology might require a special type of science education that emphasizes the great cultural and societal relevance of these fields rather than their abstract content.

Last, but by no means least, is the matter of the evolutionary context of human behavior. If basic human behavior is primarily determined by nurture, by the environment, then that behavior should reflect cultural changes in the environment that occur over a time of centuries, or even decades. In the past 10,000 years or so, since the introduction of the technology of agriculture, human beings have radically changed the cultural and physical environments they live in. From throwers of spears, they have become potential intercontinental hurlers of hydrogen bombs. From scratchers of the earth, they have become the scourges and possible destroyers of the land they till, the rivers they drink from, and the atmosphere they breathe. Has our *basic* behavior changed to respond adequately to the clear and present dangers of these developments that we have engineered? Superficialities aside, I think that the answer is no.

To be sure, the majority of people have shown themselves quite capable of acquiring difficult new skills that their ancestors of 10,000 years ago did not dream of possessing: reading and writing, or driving automobiles in Rome or Los Angeles, or sitting comfortably on bar stools (Figure 2). I suggest that these are what we earlier characterized as specific behaviors, acquired from the environment. But as far as behavioral adaptation to the larger issues of our times is concerned, the majority appear to be clueless.

Why? The conclusion seems clear to me: it is our genes that greatly influence our basic behavioral patterns, and these genes

"*So, how goes the quest for fire?*"

Figure 2. Arnie Levin from cartoonbank.com. © *The New Yorker Collection* 1996. All rights reserved.

have probably not undergone significant natural evolution in the past 10,000 years. Our inner behavioral selves have likely not changed a great deal during the time that our outer behavioral selves have shifted from learning how to hunt an animal to acquiring the means to annihilate a planet, and from the first planting of seeds to the current manipulation of the genes of living things. (This preternatural capability of modern humanity is portrayed in fable form in Appendix G.) Whereas the behaviorally influential genes of our hominid ancestors might have been suited to humans even as recently as 10,000 years ago, the same genes would have to some considerable extent now been made anachronistic. Aggressive and highly ego-centered or clan-centered behavior may have been selected for the survival of hominids and many earlier species in evolution, but it is likely to be counterproductive for the survival of modern humans, whose globally entwined culture requires a much higher level of altruistic and communal behavior than in the distant past. Further, the survival value of those gene alleles that increase human rationality and high intelligence, as well as those that increase human altruism, has within a few ticks of evolutionary time become enormous to the species. The probable low frequency of those alleles in the human population was not terribly important in the past to creatures who spent their lives hunting and gathering and fighting for dominance in the clan. Today, these conditions have changed irrevocably, but we can expect little genetic change in the human population from the comparatively slow workings of natural selection, and we can do nothing about this by genetic manipulation. Given this genetic vacuum, behaviorists must therefore rush in, realizing that because the appropriate allelic forms of the relevant genes are apparently in short supply, and because there are no means in sight to correct this genetic deficiency, the window open to nurture and direct specific human behaviors toward survival is our only possible escape route. Among what behaviorists must learn are the principles of evolutionary survival, which are the subjects of the next chapter, and how to condition humanity to grasp them.

CHAPTER 7

Life's Ancient
Strategies for Survival

Life on Earth has existed continuously for about 4 billion years.
That is an almost incomprehensibly long time. It is remarkable
enough that life could have originated spontaneously at all, but it
is even more astonishing that it has persisted for so long. After
all, the individual life is so fragile, subject to so many external and
internal traumas that are potentially fatal. Why didn't life, once
started, just peter out? Life has not only not petered out; it has
positively flourished, growing more variegated and complex over
time. It has endured through profound changes in the Earth and
its atmosphere and through catastrophic events, from bombard-
ments with planetesimal bodies to occasional collisions with gigantic asteroids. Life has been nothing if not resilient.[1] It therefore must have evolved multiple mechanisms to ensure such
long-term survival—even under the most adverse conditions—

long before humans made their late appearance on the Earth's stage. Life had been going on swimmingly (as well as aerially and ambulatorily) without humans for most of the 4 billion years. It is obviously essential, then, for us to understand these mechanisms of survival, if only to avoid inadvertently thwarting or destroying them. Here I examine just three of these survival mechanisms, which I refer to as balance, diversity, and elimination.

EVOLUTION AND THE
SELECTION OF STATES OF BALANCE

Evolution's hallmark is usually thought to be the generation of new species over time. But even more critical to survival than speciation has been the evolutionary selection of states of balance within and among living systems. At all biological levels, from individual cells to the entire biosphere, natural selection has seen to it that living systems have developed self-regulating balances of their components and activities; some balances are local, others global. Maintaining each state of balance is vital to the survival of the system that it regulates.

Consider the cell, for instance. In its interior, thousands of different chemical reactions are going on simultaneously, many competing to use the same molecules. This enormously large set of reactions must be kept in balance; otherwise, a few reactions might take over and overwhelm the entire cellular machinery. Take the analogy of a Chinese kitchen. To prepare dinner in a Chinese restaurant, the various dishes have to be cooked in the appropriate relative amounts. It would not do for the chef preparing the egg rolls to requisition most of the evening's food supplies and all the oven capacity to make only this specialty. A few days of this egg rolling and the restaurant would go under. So it is when analogously an unregulated chemical process takes over in a cell; the result is either cell death or one of the set of diseases called cancer. In the cell's normal operations, perturbations to the balance may arise, such as are produced after we eat a meal or contract an infectious disease. But these transient disturbances are self-corrected by regulatory mechanisms, and the cell's balanced state is soon restored.

At the level of organisms, balance is also an absolute necessity for survival. Animal species are often parts of food chains in the local areas they inhabit. One species preys on certain other species for its food and, in turn, other species prey on it. Clearly the various species in these food chains must be kept in balance. If a predator species consumes its prey to extinction, the predator will also become extinct. Predators avoid this fate by concentrating on weakened or older prey and on the very young, which are easier to kill, allowing the healthy adults to survive in sufficient numbers to reproduce. These processes preserve the balances among all the species of plants and animals.

Individual organisms are really living zoos, in or upon which many other kinds of organisms make their homes. These joint living arrangements usually are in a congenial and balanced state, providing important benefits to both the host and its guests. In the human body, for example, the large intestine is an entire country occupied by all kinds of bacterial immigrants who, in return for their subsistence on the nutrients surrounding them, perform many crucial functions, for example, the synthesis of vitamins such as biotin that are essential to the human host, which on its own cannot manufacture them. This is one reason why antibiotics must be taken sparingly and with care.

Another profoundly important case of balance in the global environment has to do with the ozone in our atmosphere. Ozone (O_3) is generated when the sun's ultraviolet radiation acts on the oxygen (O_2) molecules in the upper troposphere. Ozone performs the vital function of scavenging most of the free radicals that ultraviolet radiation creates in the atmosphere. These free radicals, which are highly reactive chemicals, would otherwise do a lot of damage to living systems that are exposed to the atmosphere. The damage includes causing excessive mutations in DNA, thereby producing cancers and other serious aberrations. (Avoidance of such radiation damage is no doubt why life on Earth first proliferated in the oceans. Two billion years ago, before the era when organisms evolved that could use water for photosynthesis to produce gaseous oxygen, the Earth's atmosphere did not contain oxygen. Any life on land—or on any waterless planet—would have been exposed to, and killed by, ultraviolet radiation in the absence of the ozone made from atmospheric oxygen.) Recall the ongoing furor about ozone "holes" in the upper atmosphere. These holes result from the release of free-radical-generating chlorofluorocarbons, used in refrigerating devices, into the atmosphere. These react with, and destroy, the protecting ozone. This is another example of how technological innovation can cause severe problems, often unanticipated, by upsetting a state of balance in the environment.

A crucial corollary of balance is interdependence. One cannot, for example, radically increase or eliminate one molecular component of a biochemical reaction sequence in a cell, or one animal species in a food chain, without often disturbing the entire system. Many of these interdependencies are not yet fully understood. At the organismal level, for instance, an experiment was carried out a few years ago on the genetic engineering of mice, in order to increase their content of a single gene encoding a growth factor protein. As a result, engineered mice were produced that were twice as big as their normal litter-mates. But when the experimenters tried to breed these supermice, the mice turned out to be sterile. There was no reason to have anticipated a connection between a mouse's size and its sexual function, and so this result was not only a great surprise but also a caution for those molecular geneticists, gene therapists, and plant bioengineers intelligent enough to appreciate its significance.

Such interdependence made necessary by evolution means that no single living species can survive on its own. The human species has not been selected evolutionarily to go it alone. It must discover and pay heed to the many systems of balance in which it vitally participates.

DIVERSITY AND THE ACCUMULATION OF SURVIVING SPECIES

Superimposed upon, and a crucial part of, all these balancing acts, life has slowly evolved a tremendous variety of new forms and species. As these appeared, they became incorporated into already established balanced systems, adjusting them only slightly and not overwhelming them. The modern human species is the only one that threatens to depart radically from this pattern, with consequences that, as we all should know, may well be irreconcilable with survival.

The evolutionary method of such speciation, with its accompanying adjustments of states of balance, has generally permitted the earlier species to persist. For this reason, the overall process of creation of new life forms might be termed *conservative innovation*, which in this instance is not an oxymoron. New and more complex species have arisen during evolution, by processes such as gene duplication and mutation (described earlier), as individual offshoots of existing species; the ancestral species, because they are stabilized by already established states of balance, are often not greatly disturbed by the newcomers' arrival. Bacteria were the first successful living forms from which all more complex species evolved. Yet bacteria constitute a very stable and prosperous form of present-day life, having endured for nearly 4 billion years in a slowly adjusting state of balance, despite the competition from much more complex systems. Note how different this situation is from most technological innovation in recent human social and cultural life. When, for example, the automobile was invented and made available cheaply, it finally—as the railroad had earlier begun to do—eliminated the horse-drawn carriage and the stagecoach as means of individual and family transportation. The only remnant left behind was the term *horsepower*, a ghost of the past, like the grin of the Cheshire cat.

The generation of diversity among living species really accelerated when the mechanism of reproduction, which is predominantly asexual in the bacteria, became predominantly sexual with the appearance of nucleated (eukaryotic) cells about 2 billion years ago. Sexual reproduction has allowed new species to be generated with increased efficiency in the past 2 billion years. The resulting diversity of living species is astonishing: there are millions of species of insects alone. The persistent introduction of new species during evolution has been critical, because it is estimated that 99 percent of all species that have ever existed have become extinct in response to the biosphere's slowly but continually changing environments.

Why do we have so many species? One might imagine a system of life on Earth that consisted of tens of thousands of species rather than tens of millions. If most of this vast number were in fact merely superfluous and served no purpose, it seems likely that over evolutionary time natural selection would have eliminated them. Considerable energy is required to maintain such an enormous diversity of species, including developing mechanisms to keep similar species from hybridizing with one another. If mutations arose that decreased such superfluous diversity, they would therefore have presumably conferred a selective advantage to the surviving species. This rather suggests that the great diversification of species is essential to the long-term survival of life. Ecological theorists have in fact recently suggested that greater diversity of species exerts a powerful stabilizing influence on life, making it easier for such highly diverse systems to maintain states of balance than for less diverse ones to do so.[2] Here is a very oversimplified example: if a particular species of predator can prey on many different species, rather than on only one, then the extinction of any one, or even of several, of the species of prey would not result in the extinction of the predator species. Given the very large number of localized environmental niches on Earth, within each of which a state of balance must be achieved, the existence of vast numbers of species may not be so surprising.

These ideas have considerable practical significance. Society as a whole tends to be rather cavalier about species extinctions. Why should the fate of the spotted cross-eyed owl or the white-tailed warbling gnat-catcher be of any concern to us, when their preservation leads to a loss of money and jobs in the deforestry and building industries? So what if we denude the 2,000-year-old redwood forests? If you've seen one tree, you've seen them all, right? So what if the fishing industry nets and destroys entire populations of edible fish species? There are still lots of other fish to fry, right? Most of the time, however, we do not even know whether a particular species is important to some state of balance in the environment and do not realize that its elimination may entail serious consequences.

A current case in point involves the sea otter population in North Pacific coastal areas. This population had been stabilized in recent years, thanks to the International Fur Seal Treaty, after fur traders had hunted the otters to near-extinction in the early 1900s. More recently, however, their numbers have again declined precipitously in some coastal areas, most likely because of unusual predation by killer whales. Killer whales and otters normally live together amicably in the same waters, but oceanic overfishing has depleted the food supply of the seals that the killer whales prefer to feed on. Thus the seal population has collapsed, and the whales have been forced to prey on the otters. In turn, otters feed on sea urchins, which forage kelp beds. So the decline of the otters has greatly increased the number of sea urchins, and this has led to the overgrazing of the kelp beds. Oceanic overfishing has, then, touched off extensive chains of severe transformations all the way to the coastal waters. An entire complex system that was originally in a state of balance has been convulsed by one derangement, overfishing.

The issue of forest fires provides an even more troubling instance of how we moderns have upset nature's balances—more troubling because the problem was created in the first place by our good intentions. Over the years, we have developed elaborate technology to suppress hard-to-reach forest fires. One might think that minimizing fire damage in forests could only be beneficial; unfortunately, this is not always so. Forest fires are un-avoidable, usually started by lightning. Such fires have been a part of the long evolutionary history of life on land, and their effects have therefore been incorporated by natural selection into the states of balance of forest systems. In other words, these forest systems have come to depend on occasional fires to maintain their states of balance. Suppressing all forest fires often turns out to upset the balance. As one example, the red maple tree is now taking over America's Eastern forests, driving out the oaks and elms. Occasional fires used to keep the rapidly growing but more fire-vulnerable red maple in check, but no longer. The dominance of the red maple will likely cause many animal species in these forests—including a variety of birds, nut-eating creatures, and insects that live on oak bark—to go extinct. So good intentions alone, without the required knowledge to guide them, can prove to be unreliable in environmental, as in all human, affairs.

ELIMINATION OF DEFECTIVES

Crucial to the evolutionary survival of life has been the elimination of defective forms as they have inevitably and continuously arisen as a result of mutational events. Elimination operates at every level, from the molecular to the organismal. When defective humans are eliminated by these natural selection processes, such processes may seem ruthless to us because they do not reflect human moral values, but why should they? Natural selection is really indifferent to the long-term survival of individual humans. Evolution is not focused on individual survival or even ultimately on the survival of species; rather, it is concerned with the survival of life. Therefore, when random and unavoidable mutations generate defective alleles of genes in individuals of a sexually reproducing species, such genes are usually eliminated after a number of generations because offspring bearing two copies of these genes (born of healthy parents who each bore only one defective copy) did not live long enough to reproduce and transmit them. It is estimated that each human being harbors 5 to 10 defective alleles among his or her 50,000 to 100,000 genes, kept at that level in the species by the competition between mutation and elimination. Again, we see the operation of the principle of balance.

. . .

All of these and other survival mechanisms operated spontaneously for billions of years before the advent of humans. And for almost all of the several million years of our history, we have unknowingly been an integral part of these evolutionary operations. The numbers of humans increased only very slowly during that time, limited by our ability to obtain food by hunting and gathering. The life of primitive human beings was, as Hobbes famously surmised, "solitary, poor, nasty, brutish, and short." Almost in the blink of an eye on the evolutionary time scale, however, that life changed radically. The invention of agriculture only about 10,000 years ago initiated the revolution. A plentiful and generally reliable source of food freed humans for the first time from the restraints of their prior evolutionary history. Our numbers began the rapid exponential increase that has persisted to this day, made possible by an increased food supply produced by continued advances in agricultural technology. Agriculture required humans to give up their nomadic existence and to settle on the land. Humans became the rooted plants of the animal world. From villages to towns to great city-states was a chain of transformations that then took only a few thousand years. With settled society, all kinds of marvelous new skills were developed: written languages, religions, technical achievements like the invention of the wheel and the working of metals, all part of this early flowering of human urban culture. The pace of these changes accelerated enormously in the next few thousand years, leading to the Industrial Revolution in the 1800s and today's postindustrial, technological world.

We are all enamored of this new world, rightfully impressed with its glorious achievements. Our technologically based civilization has rescued humankind, or at least the part that can enjoy it, from a hard-scrabble and mean existence and enabled many to achieve substantial comforts, some even nobility. But humankind appears to be largely blind to some of the grave problems that the same technology has increasingly thrust upon the world, particularly as these problems have proliferated in the past 100 years. They foreshadow potential disasters. These problems have arisen because throughout this entire period, starting with and including the invention of agriculture, technology has unwittingly violated, and has begun to overwhelm, the ancient mechanisms of evolutionary survival. The most egregious of these crimes against evolution (for that is what they really are, ignorance of the laws of evolution being no excuse) is that humans have overpopulated the world and continue to do so at a largely unabated pace.[3] Our numbers have leaped from a few million 10,000 years ago to over 6 billion today. Humans are no longer in balance with the world's other inhabitants; as a result, and as we are often told but do not seem to absorb, our forests are being destroyed, all kinds of species are being pushed to extinction, arable land is being denuded, resources are irreversibly consumed, and supplies of fresh water, once thought unlimited, are becoming perilously short.[4]

Incredibly enough, the technology of agriculture, one of humanity's great triumphs, has become a growing menace. From its beginnings, our practices of agriculture have unknowingly been anti-evolutionary: the *monoculture* of selected grains and vegetables—the dense cultivation of only single plant species on large plots of land—has eventually disrupted the ages-old evolutionary balance maintained by natural plant *polycultures*—varieties of plants growing adjacent to one another—with their environment. This balance within polycultures included maintaining the nitrogen cycle and the water cycle and controlling insect predation, all of which became unbalanced in the practice of monoculture. In more recent times the extensive use of fertilizers and pesticides, with their malignant consequences, has been introduced to counter the effects of some of these disruptions. The needs of irrigation have led to the damming of almost all of our formerly free-flowing rivers and to the severe depletion of our irreplaceable water aquifers. How much longer can this go on?

On another front, the technology of medicine, with its widely celebrated ability to save the lives of individuals who are genetically defective, is operating counter to the evolutionary program of natural elimination. By promoting humane medical intervention to keep genetically defective individuals alive and able to reproduce, we are gradually loading down the human gene pool with defective allelic genes. What will be the biological consequences for future generations? We do not know, but some scenarios are disturbing. On the other hand, a rational solution to the problem is available. Couples who know, from their family histories or by genetic testing, that they are at risk of having a child with a serious genetic defect can discover by amniocentesis whether the early embryo the woman is carrying has the defect and can make a decision to abort the embryo early in gestation, with the hope of later having other children without the genetic defect.[5] Likewise, medicine's gift of increased longevity, which is so widely admired, bids fair in the short run to disrupt the balance among age groups in our society and to shatter our economy if it continues unchecked (see Chapter 5).

The details of these profound and steadily increasing technological depredations of the environment and of our society would require several books by themselves. The overall implications, nevertheless, are abundantly clear. Humanity's technological commands, particularly as they have accelerated in the past hundred years, have begun to seriously compromise the slow-to-adjust natural mechanisms for the survival of life—the mechanisms of balance, of diversity, and of elimination—that evolutionary selection set in place billions of years ago.[6] No humanly created mechanisms are available to substitute for or replace them.

Look at it this way. Suppose that, indeed, "all the world's a stage," and imagine that I am thrown up on that stage only in the last ten seconds of a superb tragi-comedy that has already gone on for more than four hours and that features countless other actors involved in an intricate drama. After remaining in the background for most of my ten seconds, I suddenly rush to center-stage. Ignoring everyone and everything else, I begin at furious speed to build a gigantic robot, using parts that I gouge out of the stage sets, unaware that as a result the scenery will soon collapse on top of everyone. Naturally you would think me an extremely dangerous lunatic. That is a parable for the technological catastrophe that humans, through ignorance and arrogance, may well inflict on ourselves and the world.

The majority of us must rapidly acquire an awareness of the operations of evolution, an awareness that experts possess but seem powerless to disseminate to the general public. With this knowledge must then come the wisdom to apply it to our human, particularly technological, activities. As awesome as our technological skills have become, if they do not soon submit to the higher skill of rational wisdom, they will wreak havoc on life—and, in particular, on human life—quite possibly within only a few more generations. The will to deal rationally with these problems *now* is humanity's best hope for a civilized future.

CHAPTER 8

The Future
Prospects of Biology

In the past several chapters, I have very briefly surveyed the extensive knowledge of biological science that has been acquired in the past, especially in the past half century. What can we anticipate from biological science in the future? In view of its astonishing recent successes, is biology primed to expand its reach to much greater heights, to tackle and solve problems of still greater complexity than it has already undertaken? What might such potentially soluble problems be? Will some important biologically centered problems ultimately be intractable to scientific understanding? Of particular interest is the question of whether a rigorous and predictive science of human beings and human society will eventually be possible. As I explore these questions in this chapter, I will also have the opportunity to examine more deeply the foundations for the extraordinary success of molecular biology in our time.

These inquiries clearly require a great deal more speculation than did all of our earlier discussions about biology. In part, this chapter is a digression into the philosophy of science, which, for our purposes, must constitute only a short detour off the main track. You may choose to pass over it without losing the thread of the book's main arguments, which are grounded mainly in established facts. But exploring questions about the future of biology does raise matters of broad interest, including, for example, problems in the social sciences, even though any conclusions drawn at this time must necessarily be tentative.

There exists a very substantial literature on the philosophy of biological science and its relation to physics and chemistry.[1] To add my few thoughts to the analysis of these questions, I start by elaborating an idea mentioned earlier: that biology, in all its enormous range and diversity, must ultimately be understood as a single connected science. Biological systems can be classified into five successive levels of organization—molecular, cellular, tissue and organ, organismal, and population or societal. Molecular biology deals with chemical structures (molecules) that are so small they cannot be seen in the light microscope. Only in the twentieth century was the true nature of protein, RNA, and DNA molecules discovered. Cells, though, are large enough to be seen in the light microscope, which allowed scientists to explore cell biology in depth beginning in the nineteenth century. Objects at the next two levels—tissue and organ, and organismal—can of course be seen with the unaided eye, and thus they were the main objects of biological investigations (such as anatomy and physiology) for centuries before good microscopes became available. The fifth level is the province of evolutionary and population biology and of ecology; where investigations at this level specifically examine human society, they have been mainly the domain of the social sciences, rather than biology, up to this time.

Each succeeding level has its own special features and new problems to consider. In addition, each succeeding level, in principle at least, incorporates and organizes the entire set of previous ones. Necessarily, then, the complexity of the system increases substantially with each level. It is thus intellectually paradoxical, although physically obvious, that the more complicated levels—the tissue and organ level and the organismal level—came under study before the relatively simpler ones of cells and molecules. Recall the example of hereditary transmission (see Chapter 4), which was first studied by Mendel and others at the organismal level and which led to the concept of the gene. Only later was the gene concept brought down to the cell by microscopic investigations of germ-cell lines and of the mechanics of mitosis and meiosis. Finally, the molecular nature of the gene was discovered. It consists of DNA, a unique type of chemical molecule whose structure allows it to be faithfully replicated during the course of hereditary transmission. This example of how biological knowledge has been acquired is of general relevance. Biologists often first recognize a phenomenon at some higher level, but then in order to understand how it actually happens, they need to elucidate eventually the cellular and then the molecular events that are among the essential contributors to the phenomenon. Molecular biology, despite being the most recently developed branch of biology, is therefore at the base of the pyramid of biological science. Its nature needs to be more deeply probed.

MOLECULAR BIOLOGY AND THE CONCEPT OF FIXED FUNCTIONALITY

Chapters 4 and 5 describe some of the many important and illuminating developments in understanding life processes by means of molecular biology. The successes of molecular biology have been nothing short of astonishing, but the basis for this success has hardly been examined. Why has molecular biology worked so well? Let's take a closer look at some of the foundational ideas and assumptions behind this science.

In the tradition of Galileo and others, molecular biology is predicated on at least three materialistic concepts. The first, *the universality of the laws of physics and chemistry*, we have already analyzed in some depth. It posits that molecular biology is strictly an offshoot of the operations of the same laws of physics and chemistry that govern the rest of the universe. The second concept is one that is now well established by experiments, though a century ago it was by no means obvious: *the particularity of living systems*. In the era before molecular biology, living cells were thought to consist mainly of "protoplasm," an ill-defined and amorphous gel-like, more or less homogeneous fluid, which was all that early microscopes could discern inside cells. Modern molecular biology has proved, however, that this fluid contains definite particulate components—especially, as discussed in Chapter 4, discrete molecules of proteins, RNA, and DNA and their various molecular aggregates—all immersed in a water milieu and all bounded by a cell membrane.

The third basic concept—one that I stress in this chapter—is what I call fixed functionality.[2] This term is meant to denote *the association of a single and unique function, or closely related set of functions, with a particular structural entity*. It means that the functionality does not vary with changes in the environment but remains the same regardless, as long as the particular entity retains its characteristic structure in that environment. Though it may sound abstruse, the concept of fixed functionality carries a lot of weight. It determines whether a particular system can be successfully studied by the reductionist methods of modern science, as we explore in the rest of this chapter.

The concept of fixed functionality is so firmly embedded in the practice of modern molecular biology that it is taken completely for granted by its practitioners, but it is in fact not at all obvious, nor are its enormous consequences adequately appreciated. The concept applies especially to the proteins. It is well established that each kind of protein enzyme generally promotes one narrowly specific chemical reaction and no other. (This is why, in order to carry out all the thousands of individual kinds of reactions in a cell, so many different kinds of proteins are required.) This specific function is the consequence of the unique three-dimensional arrangement of the atoms that are linked together in a particular giant protein molecule—another instance in which structure determines function. (See Appendix A for more details.) The structure of each of these proteins is ultimately encoded in the DNA, ensuring that when the gene for a particular kind of protein is faithfully translated, exactly the same protein molecular structure, with its unique function, is synthesized in many billions of copies in a single cell.

The fixed function of proteins is even more remarkable than this, because a protein's structure is in fact not entirely rigid but is instead somewhat flexible. This flexibility is essential in controlling the balance of chemical reactions in a cell (see Chapter 7). When certain specific small molecules, called allosteric regulators, bind to particular sites on the surface of a protein enzyme molecule, its three-dimensional structure is slightly altered in a way that affects the *rate* with which the enzyme molecule promotes its characteristic chemical reaction but does not alter the *kind* of reaction that is promoted. Thus, even after such allosteric structural changes in a protein molecule are induced, its specific function is not changed; only the speed of the function is altered. Fixed functionality is maintained.

Why is it so important that the functionality of proteins be fixed? Because it is required for the success of the most basic research procedure in molecular biology. Protein molecules of a given kind (in many millions of identical copies) are isolated from the complex mixture inside living cells and placed in a water solution in a test tube. One then determines which particular chemical function each kind of protein molecule mediates. The protein function observed in the artificial milieu of the test tube can then generally be ascribed to the same molecule within its natural environment in a cell, as long as the giant molecule's unique three-dimensional structure is preserved when it is isolated. In this manner, hundreds of kinds of protein molecules have been isolated and their chemical functions identified. This procedure is a form of scientific reductionism (see Chapter 3).

Now imagine the consequences if the principle of fixed functionality did not apply at the molecular level. Suppose, for example, that the three-dimensional structure of a protein molecule was so altered by different environments that the molecule promoted a somewhat different chemical process in each environment. A given kind of protein might then have different functions in different cells and, in particular, a different function in the artificial test tube environment. For such a situation to be amenable to study, one would need to know the composition of each cellular environment with great precision in order to reconstitute it in a test tube. As this is an extremely complex problem, progress in molecular biology in the absence of fixed functionality would almost certainly have been much slower over the past 50 years.

The possibility, however, that the functionality of proteins might not be fixed is not at all unreasonable or without precedent. No one has demonstrated theoretically that fixed functionality is a necessary feature of protein molecules. Rather, it has turned out to be a fact of nature and is almost certainly a consequence of natural selection early in evolution.[3] Fixed functionality is already characteristic of the proteins in the earliest forms of life still extant on the Earth, the bacteria. On the other hand, fixed functionality at the molecular level is a very costly proposition for living systems to maintain. A large part of the information content of DNA, and much of the energy consumed by living systems, must be channeled to the production of very many different kinds of protein molecules, each carrying out only one narrowly specific chemical function. In principle, it would seem less costly to encode and produce a smaller number of proteins, each of which was adaptable to a variety of functions depending on the environment. Undoubtedly for good reasons, though, that is not the way life on Earth rapidly evolved and stabilized.

In any event, fixed functionality at the molecular level of life is the key to the enormous successes of molecular biology in our time. Without it, the application of reductionist principles for carrying out scientific research would not have been possible in molecular biology. In fact, I can be even more general than that. The extent to which the functionality of a system is fixed determines the success of reductionist science applied to that system. A question then immediately arises: to what extent is functionality fixed at the next higher level of biological organization, the cell?

FIXED FUNCTIONALITY AT THE CELLULAR LEVEL

Just as the particulate unit of molecular biology is the molecule, so the particulate unit of cell biology is the cell. Even though functionality is rather rigorously fixed at the molecular level, it is more relaxed at the cellular. A cell's signature set of functions can often be converted to another set of functions by appropriate changes in the molecular environment of the cell. Such adaptability at the cellular level is indeed crucial to the natural processes of growth and development of an organism, where cells of a more primitive type are often converted into cells with a more differentiated set of properties upon receiving certain chemical signals at appropriate times from their surrounding molecular and cellular environments. A few of these cellular changes can be reproduced in the test tube by treatment of intact cells with certain proteins (growth factors, hormones) that are thought to function similarly in the living organisms.

Another instance of environmental influence on cellular functionality is the immune response of higher organisms. Foreign substances (antigens) that enter the body can induce the modification, proliferation, and differentiation of certain cells (B and T lymphocytes, mainly) to counteract the effects of the specific antigen. This is the principal means nature has given us to fight diseases generated by viruses and bacteria from the environment. Another example of environmental alteration of cellular function is cancer, which is basically a permanent change in a cell's properties that is induced by environmental factors, such as radiation or chemical carcinogens, that modify the cell's DNA.

Fixed functionality at the molecular level, however, introduces some constants into the variability of cellular behavior. A particular kind of giant molecule can be presumed to carry out the same chemical function in cells as different as muscle cells or liver cells or brain cells. And because a specific large molecule generally has only one chemical function, its contribution to the overall economy of a cell is in principle determined solely by how many copies are in the cell and by the speed with which its unique chemical function is allowed to occur (or, as we say, is regulated) by other molecular components in that cellular milieu.

Despite departures from fixed functionality at the cellular level, it is at this level that the greatest progress in biological science can be expected in the next decades. Evidence for such progress is already abundant, deriving mainly from extension of knowledge and techniques from molecular biology to cell biology. In fact, the integrated discipline of molecular cell biology has achieved its own status and recognition in recent years.

For example, one of the most distinctive features of a cell is its membrane, the extremely thin surrounding structure that must remain intact if a cell is to survive. The membrane not only contains and confines the cell's contents but also regulates which molecules get into and out of the cell and which chemical signals are transmitted from the environment into the cell. The molecular basis for the structure and the many fixed functions of the cell membrane is now well on the way to being thoroughly understood. Another key problem of cell biology—how cell growth and division are controlled (the central problem in cancer)—is also becoming more tractable.

The rather strict adherence to fixed functionality exhibited by most biological molecules and the comparatively more adaptable functionality of cells, besides affecting the success of scientific studies of the molecular and cellular levels of biology, turn out to have major consequences for the characteristics of all life, including human. A molecule is not alive; DNA, or even aggregates of molecules, such as viruses containing proteins and DNA, is not alive. The first biological level on which autonomous life appears is the cell. Single-cell bacteria are alive; that is, in the appropriate environment they can survive and reproduce their kind autonomously. *The transition between the inanimate and living worlds therefore coincides with the transition between, on the one hand, a strict adherence to fixed functionality and, on the other, a more relaxed observance of it.* This also means that the living world is generally much less deterministic, much less readily predictable, than the inanimate world.

This blurring of determinism and predictability in living systems has a crucial bearing on, among other concerns, the problem of free will. Many thinkers, confronting modern molecular biology and its apparently deterministic implications for human life, have asked how the mechanisms of biology permit the exercise of human free will. That is, if a living human body is only a complex machine whose actions are strictly determined by mechanisms that are unresponsive to conscious decision, then presumably there is no such thing as free will. If there is no free will, then a human being has no moral responsibilities. This is therefore an acute problem in philosophy and in human affairs.

The eminent philosopher Alfred North Whitehead, in struggling with the problem, made a remarkable suggestion in 1925, long before the advent of modern molecular biology and even before we were aware of the existence of proteins.[4] To address free will, Whitehead proposed a "theory of organic mechanism." In particular, he argued that "[biological] molecules [operate] in accordance with the general laws [of physics and chemistry], but differ in their intrinsic characters according to the general organic plans of the situations in which they find themselves." In other words, molecular functions are responsive to changes in the local environment, which, under appropriate circumstances, can be signaled by thoughts from the brain. Such a mechanism could, in principle, then accommodate to the exercise of free will. In my terminology, Whitehead's proposal is that protein molecules are *not* functionally fixed; that each kind of molecule does not have a single and unique function; and that, instead, the molecule's function changes with its local environment. As we have seen, this turns out not to be the case: protein molecules are generally of fixed functionality. *But cells exhibit a much more adaptable functionality.* Whitehead's proposal, if it were centered on the cell instead of the molecule, would be tenable. Suitable chemical (molecular) stimuli are known to alter cellular functions, sometimes quite rapidly, and such stimuli could (by mechanisms as yet unknown) originate from thought processes arising in the brain. That the cell may possess more adaptable functionality than the molecule may therefore be extremely significant for the problems of moral philosophy.[5]

FIXED FUNCTIONALITY AT THE ORGANISMAL LEVEL

We next move to the level of the organism. The units of the structure of organisms are the tissues and organs. What can be said about the functionality of these units? Tissues and organs are functionally fixed to the extent that each exhibits a specific function (for example, mechanical activity by muscle tissue, electrical signal transmission by nerve tissue) and retains this function under different environmental conditions. In contrast, some tissues and organs are subject to changes in their function that are induced from the surrounding environment—for example, the changes in developing gonadal tissue induced by sexual differences between male and female and by the onset of puberty, or the manifold tissue changes induced in a mother during pregnancy. Such effects are departures from fixed functionality at the tissue and organ (and cell) levels.

The brain is an organ deserving special mention. Not only do we encounter in the brain one of the last great mysteries of organismal biology—namely, an understanding of the nature of thought and consciousness (see Chapter 4)—but in addition it is the least functionally fixed of all tissues and organs, being continually subjected to functional modifications brought about through the processes of learning and conditioning. The molecular mechanisms responsible for these changes are still essentially unknown.

Despite problems arising from adaptability instead of fixity of function at the organismal level, our deeper understanding of the molecular and cellular levels of biological science will have a growing impact on organismal biology and, especially, on medicine. Astonishing progress has been made in learning the detailed causes of genetic diseases, such as sickle cell anemia, muscular dystrophy, and cystic fibrosis. These diseases are brought about because of naturally occurring mutations in individual genes, which produce altered proteins that function defectively. Because we now know the genes and proteins that participate in creating the diseases, sophisticated therapies for them will likely be devel-

oped in the not-too-distant future. The basic molecular and cellular mechanisms of cancer are also under intense investigation,
and, during the past ten years, we have come to understand the
fundamental nature of cancer for the first time.

And it is to the knowledge of molecular and cell biology acquired in the past few decades that we turn in desperation as we
attempt to control the scourge of AIDS. Within a few years of
recognizing the disease, the causative agent, the human immuno-
deficiency virus (HIV), was identified, and the mechanism by
which it destroys the infected host's immune system was established. Despite certain complexities, the prospect of an effective
therapy based on these findings offers hope for the near future.
It is sobering to realize that had the AIDS epidemic struck at any
earlier time, even as recently as 50 years ago, little possibility of
controlling it by medical intervention would have existed. Its potential to decimate our species would have gone totally unchecked
because of the limited state of knowledge of molecular and cell
biology at the time. Shortly into the new century, however, effective means to arrest and eliminate this apocalyptic contagion
should be developed.

FIXED FUNCTIONALITY
AT THE SOCIETAL LEVEL

Now let's think about the human condition. Many of today's most
frustrating social problems would benefit greatly from increased
scientific understanding. If one accepts today's social values, what
is the optimal distribution of wealth? What is a manageable population size, and how should its flux be regulated? What forms
should education take at its various levels in order to yield maxi-

mum benefit to future generations? How can we best control drugs and substance abuse? There are a host of such issues. All of them might be addressed more scientifically than they are now if suitable methods were available and the will existed to pursue them. But we are very far from such a condition at the present time. Here we enter an intellectual territory dominated by social scientists rather than biologists. A merger of the two classes of disciplines would be a desirable development if progress is to be made in solving these human problems. This is the position strongly advocated by E. O. Wilson, the founder of the scientific discipline of sociobiology.

Since the unit of the society is the individual human being, we should then ask to what extent the characteristics of an individual are functionally fixed. Two hundred years ago, before the science of genetics was recognized, the leading figures of the Enlightenment considered each human being to be a *tabula rasa*, with equal and unlimited potentialities that could reach their zenith through appropriate education and environmental influences. According to this view, a human being was totally adaptable functionally. Despite individuality, a person's characteristics and behavior were not seen as intrinsic but were all derived externally. Genetics, however, now requires us to change this picture radically, as Chapter 6 discussed. This is one area where the biological scientist directly engages the problems of society.

To briefly review, each individual possesses a common background of genes (DNA structures) that makes him or her human rather than a member of another species. Superimposed on this common background of human genes, however, are genetic differences that make each individual unique. To the considerable extent that genes control human functions, including intelligence and other forms of behavior (Chapter 6), each of the more than 6 billion human beings on the planet therefore exhibits a fixed functionality. But as each is genetically different, each is unique and functionally different. This situation is similar to, but obviously more complicated than, the corresponding situation at the cellular level, with a considerable fraction of the 50,000 or so different kinds of human protein molecules in a given cell each having its own fixed function. Unlike an individual protein molecule, however, each human being is functionally fixed only to the extent that the genes influence human behavior. However important, genetic influences are not the only ones. Environmental factors also make significant contributions, especially through experience and conditioning. What is more, individual human beings are presumed to exhibit at least a modicum of free will, and this makes them even less functionally determinable. The reductionist scientific approach—understanding or predicting the overall response of a society to any situation that confronts it, starting from the characteristics of the individual human beings who constitute it—is rendered extraordinarily difficult by this degree of adaptable functionality of the individual.

I might extend these thoughts beyond human society to include the entire biosphere (the study of evolution and ecology), but I trust that my main point is already clear. As the biological level increases in size and complexity, from the molecular all the way to the societal, its particular structural unit becomes less and less functionally fixed. At the molecular level, different kinds of giant molecules have unique and unvarying functions. Toward the other end of the spectrum, the societal level, different individual humans can undergo changes in their functions according to what they learn and what conditioning they are exposed to. An individual human does not display a fixed set of behaviors in all surroundings and circumstances.

As emphasized earlier, fixed functionality has a great deal to do with our current ability to cope with, and derive a detailed scientific understanding of, a biological problem. The fact that we have had great success in molecular biology during the past 50 years does not necessarily mean that achieving deep understanding of successively higher levels of biological science is only a matter of time. Increasing departures from fixed functionality at higher levels enormously complicate scientific analysis by a reductionist approach. This makes a rigorous science of humankind extremely difficult to achieve.

Nevertheless, although it may ultimately be limited, considerable progress in scientific understanding at the higher levels of biological science may come about in the near term by concentrating on those features of phenomena that are indeed characterized by fixed functionality. I suggested this earlier in passing. For example, at the level of cell biology, the effect of environmental influences in changing the properties and functional behavior of cells can be traced back to the functionally fixed molecules, such as growth factors and hormones, that initiate these changes; following up on these effects, the nature of the molecular changes that result inside the cells can be investigated. In a related way, at the level of human society, the cooperative contributions of genes to individual human behavior, a subject still in its infancy, will be profitably explored as more is learned about how to analyze complex genetic phenomena experimentally. We may then be in a better position to understand the genetic underpinnings of the behavioral responses of individual humans to their environment. Pursuing their functionally fixed elements as far as possible thus provides an entree to the scientific analysis of complex and functionally adaptable systems and phenomena.

GENETIC VARIABILITY
AND HUMAN AFFAIRS

Following up this last point further, can we anticipate some of the directions in which functionally fixed elements may take our understanding of human affairs? I suggest that genetic variability within the human population will be a critical element in such analyses. I can only surmise this at present, however, because our knowledge of the genetic basis of human behavior is still rudimentary.

To incorporate genetic diversity into an analysis of human affairs, a first approach might be to consider the entire population statistically. A broadly based collection of individual behavioral characteristics treated statistically would produce a set of average behaviors for the society as a whole or for particular segments of it. But perhaps it might be more useful for some aspects of human affairs to suggest that certain rare individuals, because of their extreme genetic endowment, have an altogether disproportionate influence, for better or worse, on the human condition. For example, I propose that those individuals who possess extraordinary aggressiveness, the Attilas and Hitlers of the world, who have inordinately influenced human history, are the way they are because of their rare genetic makeup. Genetic normals, given the same circumstances, would be ineffectual as aggressors. Likewise, I believe that their rare genes have allowed those unique figures of a rational and scientific bent, the Newtons and Einsteins in the population, to have forever affected our understanding of the infinite world each of us so infinitesimally inhabits. So with the genetic extremists of a spiritual cast, the Buddhas and Jesus Christs among us, who have sought to imbue human existence with their own ethical or religious ecstasy. And those with a highly technological and inventive bent, the Gutenbergs and Edisons of the world, have changed forever the physical environment in which we live.

According to this perspective, the combined efforts of such genetically rare individuals have been disproportionately responsible for initiating the startling changes in human affairs that have brought the West in just a few millennia from a primitive agrarian society to our present-day intellectually advanced, technically brilliant, but ethically ambiguous civilization. In this view, the majority of humanity has not actively participated in the conception of this civilization. Our way of life has not been created out of the statistical average of commonplace human contributions. It is mainly the genetic extremists, greater and lesser, who have conceived and transformed the elements of our civilization; the rest of humanity has either purposefully accepted, or unknowingly and passively accommodated to, the consequences.

This analytical approach to the human condition is not likely to be popular in our society. But if it turns out to be basically sound, this view would bring an unwonted perspective not only to our past and present condition but also to our future attempts to anticipate and cope with our ever-changing civilization.

INTERACTION NETWORKS AND SCIENTIFIC UNDERSTANDING

I suggested earlier that departures from fixed functionality of the basic units of a biological system greatly impede investigations of that system by our current scientific methods. These departures have a crucial corollary. They mean that such a biological unit does not function autonomously. Instead, it must be part of, and its function substantially influenced by, *a network of interactions* with many of the other components of the system (see Chapter 7). Such networks of interactions, often large and intricate, greatly complicate efforts to analyze how the system works. This is not a new problem in science, but it is one that was deliberately bypassed in the early history of Western science. The reductionist approach largely ignores problems in which interactions among the components of a system play a dominant role. By ignoring such problems, many important matters involving large, interacting networks have not been solved; rather, they have been avoided.

The ideas behind interaction networks are best illustrated by an example. A problem of great current interest at the molecular level of biological science is the unique three-dimensional structure (that is, the detailed spatial arrangements of all the constituent atoms) of each protein molecule. These structures can be determined experimentally with high precision by X-ray crystallography, but the ability to predict them theoretically, solely from a knowledge of their constituent atoms and how these atoms are linked to one another, eludes us. The scientific details cannot appropriately be treated here, but we can say that attempts at reductionism have failed. The problem does not reduce to a summation of short-range interactions but instead requires inclusion of long-range interactions as well (that is, a large interaction network).[6] This means that many thousands of individual energy contributions between atoms that are far apart as well as close together in the protein molecule, in addition to energy interactions with the surrounding water molecules, need to be properly integrated into a structural prediction.

Furthermore, and very important, each energy contribution must be known with great accuracy if their summation is to yield the energy minimum that represents the correct structural solution. Such accuracy is beyond our present capabilities. The resulting complexity raises questions about the possibility of an ultimate theoretical solution to the problem of protein structure prediction starting from first principles. On the other hand, if we ever do learn how to predict protein structure, either theoretically or empirically, we would be able to design proteins with any desired structure and associated function. The consequences would be enormous.

At the societal level, interaction networks also play a central role in society's operations. Individuals not only contribute their own characteristic functions but also impinge upon and influence the functions of many others in the society, through family units, religious associations, and economic and political entities. The resulting networks are extraordinarily complex.

A major contribution to the empirical solution of some of these complexities, however, may be on the horizon. It involves a new and potentially revolutionary approach to the use of computers, known as massively parallel computing.[7] Until recently, high-speed computing has been designed to solve problems of a more or less *sequential* character, such as the trajectory of a missile. Massively parallel computing, in contrast, can better tackle problems of a *parallel* character, such as those encountered with network interactions. The "solution" to a problem is not necessarily presented numerically, but rather pictorially, in the form of computer graphics displaying the interaction space. This difference in representation is roughly analogous to the difference in characterizing a landscape either by a written description or by a photograph. In the written description, information about the landscape is presented in a sequential manner, as a series of words and sentences; in the photograph, the information is displayed all at once, or in parallel. Massively parallel computing will certainly be of great importance in analyzing complex problems in biological science, such as the prediction of an unknown protein structure by the empirical correlation with known protein structures.

This brief venture into the future prospects of biological science first focused on the factors responsible for the enormous successes of molecular biology in the second half of the twentieth century. I have emphasized the remarkable property of fixed functionality of the molecular constituents of all existing living systems. This property of biological molecules, such as the proteins, is not intrinsic to them but has almost certainly been selected for early in the evolution of life. At levels of biological science higher than the molecular level, from the cellular to the societal, the functions of the unit components of these systems become less and less fixed, and more and more adaptable to their environments. The consequence is that problems at these higher levels are increasingly difficult to understand by the traditional scientific method (reductionism) applied so successfully in physics, chemistry, and molecular biology during the past 400 years. In other words, the successes of molecular biology do not necessarily translate into assured future success with more complex systems. As a corollary of departures from fixed functionality, many of the most important systems in biological science involve a myriad of components that interact with one another to produce the adaptable function of the system. Such interacting networks greatly increase the complexity of a problem, but it is possible that some of this complexity can be dealt with via new approaches in computer technology. The long-range prospects for increased scientific understanding of living systems are substantial but not necessarily unlimited. Will we develop a rigorous science of humanity and human society? Because a great many difficulties must be cleared away first, the answer is probably not for a long time to come.

• • •

There is, for better or worse, more than just casual interest attached to these thoughts about the future of biological science. Molecular biology has suddenly thrust human beings into the awesome roles of Life Manipulator and DNA Redesigner, as sanctified by the U.S. Patent Office (see Appendix G). This technical ability to monkey around with evolution, however, raises a few serious questions. Do we have the scientific knowledge of the biological world, and of human beings and their societies, to undertake such technological adventures safely at this time in history? Does humanity now possess the wisdom to exercise the role of Creator? I suggest that this chapter—and the daily newspaper—provides the same answer to both questions: a resounding *no*.

Were Henry Thoreau alive today, he might offer this sage advice: "Beware of all enterprises that require new clones."

CHAPTER 9

Off with the Old Ideas, On with the New

We have covered quite a bit of ground so far. Before proceeding to new issues, it might be well to synthesize what we have confronted piecemeal in the previous several chapters.

In the past 400 years, and especially in the most recent 100, modern science has produced the greatest intellectual revolution in history. Not only that—through its technological applications, science has totally transformed our everyday physical existence. What happened that made this revolution possible? What does it all mean to humanity?

The scientific edifice that has been built over the past few centuries has stood astride two pedestals. One is the experimental method of reductionism: the isolation from the total environment of two dependent variables, or of single physical entities; studying them in the absence of any other perturbing influences; and then making the assumption that the relationships between the variables, or the properties of the physical entity, in isolation are the same as those exhibited in the total environment. As I discussed in Chapter 8, in the material world reductionism works well only when the physical entities show fixed functionality—that is, when a particular physical entity has a unique function whatever its environment. Reductionism has had, and will continue to have, enormous successes in the scientific investigation of physics, chemistry, and, more recently, molecular biology because fixed functionality is generally observed by many of the components of these disciplines. In the more complex systems of biology, however, for which functionality can vary with the environment and in which there arises the critical involvement of interaction networks, severe limits may be placed on what reductionist practice can achieve in the scientific understanding of how these complex systems operate.[1] This applies to the science of human beings and society.

The second pedestal on which modern science stands is the tremendous extension of the range of human perception that has been generated in the recent past. Prior to modern science, all of our information about the world was derived through our unaided senses, especially through visual perception. This visual perception, accomplished by means of a wonderfully complex visual apparatus, extending from the eye through several stages of processing to the higher levels of the brain, arose and was refined by evolutionary development and natural selection through the successive stages of the animal kingdom. The most obvious of the *absolutely crucial functions of this apparatus* were to enable animals to see and capture prey, especially moving prey; to escape predators; to avoid obstacles and escape other dangers; to find shelter when necessary; and to help descry appropriate mates to reproduce the species. To discharge these vital functions, natural selection has seen to it that the visual apparatus allows higher animals, including humans, to perceive *the real world out there, not some virtual one.* Chasing down a real fawn keeps a real lioness and her cubs actually fed rather than virtually hungry. While we are far from fully understanding how the visual apparatus accomplishes this, accomplish it it must. What we perceive of the world is of course limited by the range and capacity of our visual apparatus, and hence many of the detailed features of our surroundings escape our attention. But to the extent that we are permitted to see, it is the real world and not some virtual one that we become aware of.

Philosophers, approaching the problem of perception in the abstract and insulated from any biological and evolutionary insight, have often puzzled over the reality of what we perceive. Some, like Bishop Berkeley, have gone so far as to question whether a real world even exists apart from our human mind and perception. This egocentric conceit, however, makes no sense biologically or physically. Samuel Johnson had it right when he pointed out that it was very likely to have been a real rather than a virtual rock on which one had stubbed one's toe, because it hurt like the devil. To be sure, the visual system can occasionally be fooled into believing a virtual image to be real, as, for example, when we think we see a body of water that appears to lie ahead of us on a highway. But this deception is only transient; as we proceed on the highway, we perceive that the image was a mirage. The real world, on the contrary, persists. The simple biological fact is that higher animal life could not have survived otherwise than by perceiving the real world.[2]

But we see directly only those aspects of the real world permitted by the physical limitations of our human visual apparatus. Things are seen with the unaided eye only if they emit or reflect radiation within a very narrow range of the electromagnetic spectrum (which we call light) and only if they are suitably contrasted with their background. This narrow range is prescribed by the visual pigments in the rod and cone cells of the retina of the eye, which are sensitive only to such light. Humans do not see X-rays, ultraviolet or infrared radiation, microwaves or radio frequencies (that is, well over 99 percent of the electromagnetic spectrum) and were therefore entirely unaware of the existence of such phenomena as recently as 150 years ago. Likewise, our perception of distance is limited by the stereoscopic analysis provided by our two eyes and brain so that, for example, we cannot discriminate astral distances; to us, all the visible stars appear to be located on a single canopy in the night sky, much as we see them projected on the roof of a planetarium. We cannot distinguish with the unaided eye between a distant galaxy containing billions of stars and a nearby single star in our own galaxy, since both appear to us as single points of light. Thus we realized that galaxies existed outside the Milky Way only early in the twentieth century, after powerful spectroscopic telescopes were directed toward the sky.

These limits on our perception are further examples of the functional economy of evolution. Natural selection is parsimonious. It selects only for qualities that are important for survival. Our ancestors did not need to recognize objects at very long distances in order to capture prey or to avoid predators, and in view of the curvature of the Earth's surface, our ability to perceive long distances horizontally was in any event proscribed. In a similar vein, we did not need to, and therefore did not, see objects that are less than about 0.1 mm in size. The entire world of micro-organisms was therefore invisible to us and remained unknown until microscopes were invented. (Imagine his utter astonishment when Anton von Leeuwenhoek in the 1680s trained his early microscope on some tooth scrapings and discovered the Brave Old World of life, the bacteria!)

Furthermore, our perception of motion is only of relative motion. It therefore naturally appears to us that both the sun and the moon circle the stationary Earth. We are also unaware of being in motion if we move at constant velocity, and so we cannot directly sense the translation or rotation of the Earth. It is shocking how our perceptions of reality can sometimes betray us.

What the human mind has achieved through modern science, mostly in only the latest 100 of our several million years on Earth, has been to sweep away all these limitations on our perception and imagination, thereby revealing the real universe in all of its astonishing dimensions and sublimity. In this process of enlightenment, science has disclosed to humanity its true status and condition in that universe.

Modern humanity has long considered itself the protagonist on the world's stage. Any qualms we humans might have felt about the possibility that there was a significance to the universe independent of and superior to us we assuaged by inventing religions and gods that confirmed human beings as the centerpiece of Creation. Now reflect upon what science has so far wrought. Its supreme achievement, the deciphering of the reality that exists autonomously outside of ourselves, has been to teach us that neither we nor the Earth we occupy is at the center of all existence, but, on the contrary, both are infinitesimals on the very edge of physical significance in the universe. What a falling off is there!

We now *know* that Man is *not* the measure of all things, although overwhelming ego keeps urging us to think so.

But after this abject diminuendo, there comes a surging crescendo. Human beings are by far the most complicated, remarkable, confounding, and fascinating prodigies in the entire universe, as far as we know. Human capacity to probe and understand the reality of this universe is surely one of the most marvelous features of the entire cosmos. (As Emily Dickinson surmised, "The brain is wider than the sky...") Human life may be an accident in the universe, but it is a glorious one. Human love is not outshone even by the searing brilliance of a lifeless star, nor is human despair fathomed by the unfeeling depths of a black hole. Human consciousness is the richest treasure in the universe. What piece of the universe but a human being is even aware of the brilliance of a star or the enormous power of a black hole, let alone able to probe their secrets? Who but us can weave a symphony, or forge a poem, or "see a world in a grain of sand / And a heaven in a wild flower"? This reality of our brain and our consciousness, not some fantasy about our divine Creation, is what gives humanity its extraordinary significance in the cosmos.

We have discovered (although we have great difficulty truly comprehending it) that the universe contains vastness of space and time that utterly dwarfs us "cabined, cribbed, confined" mortals. We have learned of the yin and yang of energy and matter and of many, if not yet all, of the laws that govern the structures and operations of the entire universe. There is only one set of laws for everything, including life. Newtonian physics' union of the laws controlling the Heavens and Earth and modern biology's union of the laws governing animate and inanimate nature make for a singleness of all things in the cosmos, great or small, living or not. Life is astonishing, but it is not a miracle of a divine Creation. And we have come to realize that Heraclitus must have been one of the greatest geniuses of all time, for, even though he was surrounded by the apparently unchanging Heavens and Earth, he intuited correctly 2,500 years ago that "there is nothing permanent except change." The universe is indeed forever changing and expanding. Cataclysmic events continuously modify the galaxies; new stars form, old ones decay and undergo massive destruction. The universe evolves, as do all things in it.

But this knowledge of the immense structure and prodigious operations of the universe, while leaving us awestruck and bewildered, has not of itself provided us with any sense of a grand purpose to this universe and life within it. Science has revealed the grandeur and left us with the meaninglessness of existence. The true rationalist recognizes that there is no real alternative but to accept this. Others often find it entirely unacceptable and even terrifying; without a god to provide meaning to the universe and to life, their own existence is empty and a void. I have never understood why simply affixing a name to the admittedly Unknowable—be it God, Jehovah, Allah, or Mazda—constituted an explanation of anything, let alone the mystery of the meaning of the universe. The practice of naming something that is not understood is one of our oldest psychological tricks to hoodwink ourselves into believing that we have made the unknown familiar.

On our own planet, the superb structure and organization called life has arisen. One cannot be other than amazed and overwhelmed by this brilliant gem having crystallized from the cosmic dust. Early on, special giant chemical molecules like the proteins and DNA evolved to perform the chemical functions necessary for life at ordinary temperatures; these molecules became organized into a complex network inside a cell, generating from inanimate matter a living state, capable of reproducing itself and ultimately of evolving into that marvel, *Homo*. Life has proved to be enormously sturdy, but the individual life is of necessity terribly vulnerable and inescapably mortal, subject to the harsh demands of the laws and operations of physics and chemistry.

The sturdiness of life, which has permitted it to survive and prosper for 4 billion years, depends on the operation of at least three basic evolutionary mechanisms: the establishment of states of balance within collections of biological entities, from the molecules in the cells to the organisms in the biosphere; the preservation and continual generation of diversity, both within single biological species and among them; and the elimination of defectives, from the molecule to the individual organism to the species. During most of humanity's several million years on the planet, we have been absorbed unawares into these evolutionary schemes. But in the most recent past, our extraordinary technological achievements, starting with the introduction of agriculture 10,000 years ago, have allowed us to make a sudden leap forward and have led us to unwittingly isolate ourselves from these evolutionary operations. Widespread ignorance and massive violations of the ways and means by which evolution has long protected life from extinction do not bode well for the future.

The science of genetics—and especially its most recent branch, molecular genetics—has illuminated some of the great mysteries of life. It is hard to believe that a whole human being can be contained in, and transmitted by, a microscopic speck, the single-cell zygote. Further, it is absolutely incredible that all the instructions for generating a new human being are contained in a few strands of an infinitesimal molecular tape inside that zygote, a tape so thin that it requires the most powerful electron microscope to visualize it. Talk about miniaturization! This tape makes a modern computer chip assembly look like a tennis court. And with what complete astonishment must one greet the additional news that a detailed molecular understanding of how all this works has to a considerable extent been achieved and that the remainder will surely be attained in the near future!

The Rosetta Stone of life is the gene, which consists of DNA, the chemical substance of the molecular tape just discussed. Inherent in the chemical structure of DNA is the capacity of self-replication and, in addition, of encoding the information to produce all the protein molecules necessary to perform the chemical functions of living systems. All the many responsibilities for life's functions are thrust upon this miniscule amount of inanimate, but exquisitely organized, matter.

The genes, through the functioning of the proteins they encode, exercise enormous control over all living systems, including human beings. Although it is not yet known in detail how the genes cooperate to do this, it is clear that they do. This is apparent, for example, in the remarkably detailed physical similarity of two identical twins, who are separately developed clones containing identical sets of genes. We have learned that the genes program the physical structure of living forms down to the minutest details. The genes also have considerable influence on the mental structures and potential mental and behavioral characteristics of human beings. We are hardly the completely free agents that many of us have come to think we are. However, it is not an all-powerful omnipotent God, nor the confluence of the stars on the day we were born, that regulates our most basic characteristics and determines who we really are and what we become; it is primarily our genes. The evidence suggests that the environment plays an important but secondary role compared to our genetic makeup in influencing our most fundamental behaviors. That is not to say that we are mere puppets tethered to and manipulated by invisible strings of DNA. We can exercise our free will by deciding for ourselves whether to have corn flakes or eggs for breakfast. Our genes are most likely not involved in that decision. However, although we may be unaware of it, our choice of a life-long companion to share our breakfasts with us is probably substantially influenced by our particular genetic makeup and how it determines the balance of rational and irrational elements involved in making the choice. (The ancient wisdom quoted in *The Merchant of Venice* has it that "hanging and wiving goes by destiny.") It is likely that we are free to decide whether to go to the beach on Saturday or on Sunday. But whether we decide to go to the beach or to the library, which may seem to us to be entirely a free choice, is perhaps swayed by our genetically influenced predispositions.

As we learn more and more about biology—and we have really only just begun—the relevance of that knowledge to human affairs will become increasingly apparent to the general public. The prospects for the extension of biological science into an ever-wider arena was the theme of the previous chapter. I concluded that these prospects are significant but not necessarily unlimited. Promoting the progress of biological science and the awareness of the general public to its relevance in human affairs are two of the key responsibilities of rationalists to themselves and to society. As E. O. Wilson foresees: "To chart our destiny means that we must shift from automatic control based on our biological properties to precise steering based on biological knowledge."[3]

CHAPTER 10

Our Dual Worlds
The Concept of Complementarity

We have arrived at what I consider for rationalists to be the heart of this book, approaching the goal set at the end of Chapter 1. We have now explored our external world in some depth, first penetrating the mists of society's irrational anthropocentric fantasies about that world and then traversing the highways and byways of rationality and modern science. The large question that now confronts us is this: given what we know, how should a rationalist perceive and direct his or her everyday life? How can *both* our internal and external worlds be subsumed and merged into our experience?

In the past, and for irrationalists of the present, our egocentric internal world, together with an anthropocentric view of our external world derived entirely from this egocentric perspective, provided for most people a unified, coherent, and comforting philosophy of life. In that worldview, human beings are exalted to the center of Creation, set there by an omnipotent God to protect and to judge them. If one has faith in God, and behaves, one will be among the chosen on Judgment Day, to enjoy an immortal afterlife in God's Heaven. Very satisfying. It seems a shame that it is all a fiction. In view of this promised glory, perhaps some would even maintain that where "ignorance is bliss, 'tis folly to be wise."

This is not the direction a rationalist can take. What has the scientific view of the external world to offer, however? To all appearances, not much. That view appears to render each human being alone and insignificant in a meaningless universe, "his time a moment, a point his space." Rather a dismal view from our egocentric perspective, and quite unsettling to boot.

And then there is all the pressure from the vast irrational majority and its overwhelming social, political, and religious apparatus to induce conformity. The anthropocentric worldview of the West—after nearly 2,000 years of cradle-to-grave indoctrination; with the unspeakable horror of a one-way ticket to Hell and eternal damnation looming for unbelievers come Judgment Day; with the glittering allure of the greatest accumulation of untold treasures of gold, silver, precious jewels, and objets d'art in the history of the world; with the siren call of voluptuous ritual derived from the occult traditions of a pagan past; and with the stunning spectacles of magnificent cathedrals reaching for the Heavens—is difficult indeed to resist. Even for the most rational, the full-throated passion of a cathedral performance of Handel's *Messiah* or that first glimpse, in the semi-darkness of the Scuola di San Rocco, of the divine Tintorettos celebrating the Passion story could alone almost turn the trick. There are, after all, few comparable hymns or canvases dedicated to the Goddess of Reason.

It is not surprising, therefore, that the scientific view of the external world has by and large had very little impact on the broad base of the human experience. Many rational people who recognize the logical inadequacies of the anthropocentric view of the external world and have an understanding of the scientific view nonetheless put the latter view of reality aside in an inactive compartment of their minds, where it has little influence on their everyday lives. Many rationalists unthinkingly conform to the irrational mores and rituals of their society. In J. V. Cunningham's words, they "have erased the mind / As mendicants who see / Mimic the blind." Irrationalists, if they encounter the scientific view of the world, are often simply invulnerable to it. They find illusions much simpler and more palatable than reality. The truth is, however, that only the scientific view of the world corresponds closely to reality; the anthropocentric worldview is mostly just fantasy: piety in the sky. (The fact that more than 90 percent of the Western world subscribes to the anthropocentric view doesn't make it any less a fantasy. There was a time when most people also believed that the Earth was flat; in fact, the Flat Earth Society in California still claims 1,500 members.) Furthermore, the acquisition of the scientific view of the world has been the most prodigious achievement of the human mind. To have fathomed the universe and the hidden treasures of life arisen from the dust is a gift that dwarfs even that of Prometheus. To shunt the scientific view of the world aside, rendering it irrelevant to us, is to trivialize it, just as the Church trivialized Copernicus's heliocentric system when he originally published it. It is the greatest of all indignities to our essential humanity; it is now to be less than completely human.

The scientific view of the external world must reside at the core of the examined life.

On the other hand, a life devoted exclusively to contemplation of the external world is a life divorced from reality, and impossibly inhuman. Therefore, the egocentric view of our interior world and the scientific view of the external world must be brought together into a meaningful and functional philosophy of living for thinking human beings. This is not easy, because the two views appear in many respects to be either irreconcilable or, at best, unconnected. The egocentric view deals with everyday life: with friendship and love; with the birth, raising, and education of children; with the provision of food and drink; with the satisfactions of labor and career; with the enjoyment of the beauty of nature, art, and music; and with many other basic human needs and passions. The scientific view of the world appears, superficially, to have no bearing on these matters, instead dealing largely with abstract infinities and generalities of no apparent relevance to one's everyday life. That life is usually consumed by the personal and the mundane. What does the existence of a galaxy have to do with one's going to sleep hungry?

The resolution of this apparent incompatibility seems to require that a rationalist accept a fundamental duality governing human existence. On the one hand, there is an individual's internal world; and on the other, there is the scientific view of the external world. These two views of existence are effectively autonomous, existing side by side—*but* both have distinct contributions to make to a rational perception of life.

I believe that a rational way out of this paradox exists. Of special relevance to the scientifically oriented, and of interest to thinking people in general, there is an area of physics that may provide a metaphor or logical precedent for such a *necessary* duality. Usually in modern science one seeks a single, or unified, theory to explain the various phenomena observed in the universe, as when Newton unified the physics of the Heavens and the Earth. But in the case of phenomena associated with light, contemporary physics recognizes not a single, but a dual, explanation of light's properties. This involves the so-called wave-particle duality and the concept of complementarity. Certain properties of light, such as diffraction phenomena, require light to exhibit wave character. Other properties, however, such as those that arise in the interaction of light and matter, were recognized in the early 1900s to require light to consist of particulate units (photons). These latter properties cannot be explained by a wave character of light. This duality is not a temporary situation resulting, for instance, from an incomplete theory of light; rather, it appears to be a permanent state of affairs. Both wave and particle descriptions of light are correct, but each applies only to distinct subsets of light's properties that do not overlap. And this applies not only to light. Louis de Broglie in 1925 astonished the world of physics by predicting that electrons would also exhibit wave properties in addition to their previously known particle character; subsequently, this was verified experimentally and became the basis for the development of the electron microscope. It was also the key idea in the wave mechanical quantum theory developed by Erwin Schrödinger. This wave-particle duality is the origin of the general concept of complementarity, championed by Nils Bohr, a concept whose value has also been suggested in areas other than physics.

Exactly what is complementarity, and why might it be relevant here? Bohr suggested in 1927 that in order to understand the *whole* nature of light, we should not attempt to reconcile the two irreconcilables of wave and particle descriptions but rather should accept their dual essentiality and complementarity. Each description is correct, but each is only part of the story. However, the two descriptions occupy distinct and nonoverlapping domains of observations (experiments); nothing in one domain can contradict anything in the other, since the two domains are completely separate.[1]

As Bohr rather tentatively proposed some years later,[2] complementarity may also be a useful concept in areas other than physics. Its extension to cultural matters involves the realization that certain cultural phenomena necessarily require a dual explanation if they are to be adequately understood. The dual elements must be equally valid, but each should apply to different and nonoverlapping aspects of the phenomenon. One of the dual elements cannot therefore contradict aspects of the other.

The egocentric view of our inner world and the scientific view of our external world may, I suggest, be complementary views of human life, in the sense just described. The egocentric view is that one's life is an incredible gift, with all its joys and miseries. It is to be indulged in and savored and, when the time comes, given up with gratitude and a muted reluctance. But that is not all there is to human life. The scientific view of the external world is that each human being is not alone but instead is part of a great saga of existence. The atoms of our bodies have been derived from stellar decay in the galaxies that may have occurred billions of years ago. And when we die, our genes and atoms will furnish the bodies of the future. That is our true immortality. The genus *Homo* represents the latest branch of a continuous chain of life that began on earth 4 billion years ago. A rational human being cannot live life narcissistically; one's external reality is the past, present, and future world. In other words, whereas an egocentric view of one's inner world is embodied in Descartes's aphorism "I think, therefore I am" (that is, my awareness of myself establishes that I exist), the scientific view of the external world leads to its complement, "I link, therefore I am" (that is, I exist only because I am a component part of the history of the universe). One's life is not an isolated mystery, with no bonds to a past or a future. Nor is it beholden to some mythical deity. On the contrary, each human life—no less than a star's—is an integral part of a real and gloriously complex universe, with near infinities of time and space surrounding and connected to it.

The inner egocentric and the external real worlds of human beings are therefore complementary. Neither by itself adequately defines a human life; both are indispensable to it. The two worlds do not overlap; they occupy distinct domains. And one world must not contradict what is in the other's domain.

Clearly, the internal and external worldviews contribute different, and equally vital, ethical principles to one's life. The egocentric domain emphasizes the ethics of personal happiness and fulfillment, devoted to selfhood and individual survival. In this personal ethics, consideration for others is only a way of ensuring protection for one's self. The complement to this, the external worldview, is concerned with an ethics that is consonant with the preservation and enhancement of life on Earth, an ethics that is outer-oriented and future-oriented. We are each of us a link in the chain between past and future. The rights of life, liberty, and the pursuit of happiness are not only the rights each of us demands for ourselves; they are the rights as well of generations waiting to be born, for a long time to come. Those future rights must not be abrogated by present-day self-indulgence and absence of an ethical vision. Rationality is the gift that allows us to realize that there is such a thing as the future, one that extends beyond next year.

These rationally inspired ethical ideas, which I consider to be corollaries to the modern scientific view of the external world, are clearly of the greatest moment. They can contribute to a social ethics for the workings of human society that, while vastly different in spirit, is similar in consequence to the ethics espoused by traditional religions. As I have mentioned earlier, traditional religions, by providing, however irrationally, a sense of a grand purpose to all existence, have simultaneously enjoined a code of moral behavior upon the members of society to govern their everyday dealings. The belief, for example, that God created and rules the universe and everything in it for His purposes requires that His disciples in their daily lives obey and foster God's will, as revealed in the teachings of the religion's sacred texts. Thus, scripture and church leaders direct believers to love their fellow beings, even their enemies, as equal children of God; to behave honorably and fairly toward their neighbors; and to exercise the dominion humans have been given over the material world in trust from God, in support of His good will toward the Earth's present and future inhabitants and their ultimate salvation. And so, for example, Martin Luther, surrounded on all sides by the German banking and financial dynasties—the Fuggers, Hochstetters, Haugs, Meutings, Inhofs, Welsers, and so on—repeated medieval church doctrine on the matter of prices: "A man should not say, 'I will sell my wares as dear as I can or please,' but 'I will sell my wares as is right and proper...Because thy selling is a work thou performest to thy neighbor, it should be restrained within such law and consciences that thou mayest practice it without harm or injury to him.'"[3]

As we have seen, however, modern science, having abandoned the traditional religious view of a purposeful universe ruled by a benevolent deity, has substituted for it a secular universe whose purpose is unfathomable and whose outlook is primarily materialistic. Although this exorcism of purpose has been crucial for our success in obtaining a scientific understanding of material existence (Chapter 3), it has unfortunately contributed to the degradation of the social ethics of modern society. The depreciation of the religiously inspired sense of purpose and service in everyday life has permitted a largely selfish and materialistic outlook to come to dominate the life of Western society. The quasi-religious precept of "the greatest good for the greatest number" has effectively been supplanted today by "the greatest good for Number One, Me." An individual's own unlimited material prosperity has become the dominant concern of modern life, while the ethical treatment of the collective society and its future needs has become largely subordinate (Chapter 11). The medieval church's concept that riches exist for humankind, not humankind for riches, has been stood on its head.

The scientific view of the external world, however, offers much more than this ethically myopic and wholly materialistic approach to human affairs. The scientific view requires a social ethics based on intelligence and altruism if we, and certainly if our descendants, are to survive in the complicated and perilous world we have inherited. Rationality compels altruistic rationalists, just as Christianity exhorts its believers, to be concerned as much about others' interests as our own, if for no other reason than to avoid intolerable conflicts in our nuclear-armed world. Likewise, rationality dictates that, in our technological dominion over the world around us, we must make our prime objective to limit and direct our technology so as to preserve and enhance that world for present and future human society.

I suggested in Chapter 2 that the complementary joining of the scientific outer world with the egocentric inner world can provide to a rationalist some of the satisfactions that traditional religions often bestow on their irrationalist believers. In particular, as just discussed, that scientific view contributes a profound ethical approach to life and to society; it also supplies the understanding to cope with the mysteries of the world and the overwhelming forces of nature; and, further, it gives a deep if transitory significance to each human life as part of an astonishing universe. As for religion providing spiritual rapture to its believers, nonbelievers have many other channels to find the equivalent. For those who love music, "the speech of angels," the likes of a grand performance of the *Eroica* or a Milstein recording of the Second Partita can afford a superabundance of rapture, as much as one can endure. What the scientific view does not overtly furnish are the consolatory functions of traditional religions. In place of these functions, a rationalist must rely on inner strength and thoughtful harmony, which are often among reason's most characteristic companions. Life operates by chance. God does not play dice, in Einstein's famous phrase; but Life often does. Traditional religions assure their believers that everything that happens, even to the fall of a sparrow, is God's will. God is just. If one suffers, one must have deserved the suffering. The scientific view of the world, however, is far less neat and orderly. Tragedy blindly lurks; it can befall the innocent.

Cultural complementarity also can contribute to the realm of aesthetics. The argument is often made that science diminishes us, substituting cold, gray reason for the warm, vibrant imagination inherent in myth and religion, and that by concentrating on physical facts and numbers, science brutally rejects the finer values of feeling and beauty. This assumes, however, that the human approach to aesthetics must be unitary, that only one or the other of these views must predominate. Cultural complementarity rejects this dismal picture. Our egocentric inner world is the seat of our emotions, our delight in beauty, and our sense of wonder. It is autonomous, independent of and undiminished by the scientific view of the external world to which it is complementary, as long as the inner world does not maintain as fact something that the scientific world has discarded as fiction. The scientific fact that a rainbow results from the refraction and reflection of the sun's rays as they pass through droplets of water after a rain does not detract in any way from our fascinated delight at a rainbow's gorgeous beauty—but it does reject the Biblical explanation of the rainbow as a sign of divine mercy or its association with the goddess Iris by the Greeks. The trance one enters upon listening to Walter Gieseking's demonic performance of the *Tempest* Sonata is in no sense disturbed by a scientific knowledge of the wave nature of sound or the mathematical properties of harmonics. Instead, the trance and the knowledge represent two complementary, nonoverlapping ways of absorbing a musical masterpiece. One way does not exclude the other; on the contrary, one complements and often completes the other. And after we learn all that we can about the mechanics of life, we will in no way have diminished our astonishment at its magical enigmas.

Cultural complementarity can also provide a conduit between the sciences and the humanities, whose growing insulation from each other was described and deplored by C. P. Snow in his famous lecture "The Two Cultures."[4] Unfortunately, the type of insulation involved, more like lead than glass, appears to allow heat but not light to flow between the practitioners of the two cultures. (This is nothing new. For example, in *Gulliver's Travels*, Jonathan Swift judged the equine inhabitants of the Land of the Houyhnhnms to be far superior to the mathematicians and scientists of the island of Laputa—that is, he even put the horse before Descartes.) A major part of the problem for humanists is the failure, stemming from either incompetence or unwillingness, to discriminate between science and technology; the conflation of the two results in tarring the knowledge acquired by science with the brush of technological exploitation. There may be legitimate reasons for the humanities to express hostility toward much of modern technology and its often inhumane consequences; however, those reasons do not apply to the sciences themselves, which are devoted to the acquisition of knowledge, not artifacts. Humanists also often claim that much current scientific work is not terribly original or insightful; and, in particular, they disapprove of the limited vision of some of the practicing scientists they encounter. However, as they would not evaluate the condition of modern poetry from an inspection of the contents of greeting cards, so they should not judge science by its less-than-brilliant practitioners and their productions. (See Chapter 11.) What Paul Gauguin said of art applies exactly to science as well: "[It] is either plagiarism or revolution."

I view the humanities and the sciences as different, nonintegrable aspects of human intellection; they are not parts of a seamless whole, nor are they completely unconnected. Instead, they make up a duality of two complementary parts, in much the same way that our egocentric internal world and the scientific view of our external world are complementary. The humanities mostly explore our inner world, trying to illuminate the complexities of our everyday behavior, our relationships with other humans, our emotions, our responses to artistic expression, and so on. Humanists are fascinated by the extravagant diversity of life, by "all things counter, original, spare, strange." They generally want to see our existence as a magnificent whole that is more than the sum of its parts. The sciences are concerned more with the abstractions and near-infinities of our external world and seek to find an underlying unity that is obscured by this diversity. Modern science has thrived by deconstructing reality into its component parts. Humanists are drawn by the disorder of life, scientists by its order. Disorder and order: both are of the essence of existence. Neither is sufficient by itself.

Rather, therefore, than accept the simple-minded view that they are antagonists, we should recognize that the humanities and the sciences are dual and complementary aspects of human intellectual activity and understanding. The assignment of the value of a theorem in topology relative to the value of an abstract Kandinsky is clearly a meaningless exercise. It makes no sense to elevate one or the other above its cultural complement; rather, it is more sensible for each thinking person to understand both and to apply each in its appropriate domain. And there's the rub. Too few comprehend both domains, and many are evidently terribly defensive about their own. Probably nothing much will change unless and until enough individuals encompass both realms. But that seems to be becoming an ever more remote possibility, as scientific knowledge and artistic expression continue to proliferate independently, and our individual grasp of them becomes continually more fragmented. Yet, there is so much more to say. Confronted incessantly with marvels—with a brilliant night sky or the birth of a perfect child—we are surrounded by the ineffable, the wondrous strange. To have the plenary courage to search these mysteries, as the best of our scientists must have, is eminently worthy of respect. Wordsworth wrote of Newton, "...a mind forever / Voyaging through strange seas of thought, alone." This audacity, this unrelenting force of mind, should be celebrated and esteemed, most of all by humanists.

There is another inherent element of communion between the sciences and the humanities: the exercise of *intuition*. The role of intuition in science is difficult to clarify for several reasons. For one, it appears to introduce the irrational into the pursuit of science; for another, true intuition is a rare talent among scientists, most of whom would therefore not acknowledge its significance to scientific investigation. But the best scientists have it and rely on it. Intuition arises early on in a scientific study. It is insight based on an uncommonly deep understanding of the modicum of facts that usually represent all that is available at such an early stage; it is an unconventional, but not arbitrary, ability to discern connections among these facts. This intuition, this capacity to see things that others do not, is a quintessentially humanistic trait that is shared by our most original scientists and our greatest artists and poets.

• • •

In summary, rationalists are confronted with two disparate and apparently incongruous views of our existence, the view from our internal and mental world and the scientific view of the external and material world. As different as these views are, for a true rationalist they must be happily married to each other to understand and cope with the totality of existence. A precedent exists in physics for dealing with such an irreconcilable duality: the wave-particle duality of light and other quantum mechanical entities. Here, both wave and particle theories are correct, and both are essential in order to understand fully the phenomenon of light. But these views apply to separate and nonoverlapping domains of experiments, and each is inviolable within its domain. This is the concept of complementarity. In applying this concept to the social world, we refer to cultural complementarity. Cultural complementarity provides a credible and rational means of bringing together the two apparent irreconcilables: our egocentric internal world and our external world whose reality has been delineated by modern science. One should live one's life to the fullest, open to fragrance and frost, bird song and brass, poetry and pain. That is the egocentric, selfish domain. But at the same time, one's life is not a miniature universe isolated unto itself. It is indissolubly linked with the Great Universe, with its inanimate and living things, with its present, past, and future. That is the external, unselfish domain. To a rationalist, both domains are essential and complementary. Each domain invokes a distinct set of ethical principles and moral behaviors for an individual: for the egocentric domain, an ethics centered on self-fulfillment and personal happiness; for the external domain, an ethics devoted to the welfare of the whole society and, ultimately, to the very survival of life on Earth.

Cultural complementarity can also make sense out of other apparently discordant dualities, such as the relationship between the humanities and the sciences, where conflicts have arisen because many insist on a unitary instead of a dual and complementary view. In fact, whereas science generally strives for a unitary explanation of a phenomenon, it seems that human affairs often naturally lend themselves more to a dualistic or, better, a complementary understanding. This is because human affairs so often juxtapose the dual interests and characteristics of the inner self and those of the external other.

Cultural complementarity, however, is *not* simply a passive simultaneous tolerance of two opposing views, with their conceptual conflicts blithely ignored and left unresolved. Cultural complementarity provides rules for accommodating dual views: in particular, a subject that is resolved within the one domain where it properly belongs cannot be contradicted within the other domain. Traditional religions cannot be complementary to the scientific view of the external world because, as discussed earlier, their dogmas of the Creation and an afterlife have no objective reality and flatly contradict the domain of scientific knowledge; they are therefore incompatible with it.

CHAPTER 11

Rationalists in an Irrational World

Up to this point, I have concentrated mainly on the special world of rationalists and have not had much to say except in passing about the operations of the real world in which they live. In this last chapter, however, I address more directly the nature of that real world, about which, I warn you, my views run contrary to the conventional. My purpose is to consider how rationalists might come to understand the real world more clearly. The hope is that such understanding will lead to a more effective engagement of rationalists with their society, for engage they must. However much some may disdain the flagrant irrationality of this world, there is no other. No utopia has ever worked well for any extended period, and the life of a hermit in the desert has never had much epicurean appeal. So too, escape into drugs or drink is only a form of self-immolation.

In my experience, some rationalists of an altruistic bent cope with their social environment by regarding their rationality not as a rare gift but as a commonplace, a very ordinary human characteristic. Such rationalists, upon encountering the intense everyday irrationality of the world, assume that the people who, out of patriotic or religious fervor, can be persuaded to enthusiastically maim and kill their erstwhile neighbors, or who go on a mindless rampage when their soccer team either wins or loses a match, or who are encouraged to spend billions on booze or gambling rather than pay one cent in taxes, do these things only because they have been undereducated or otherwise deprived or have been placed under extreme personal stress. If these unhappy conditions were ameliorated, these people would behave more rationally, so this conceit goes. To such altruistic rationalists, "do unto others as you would have them do unto you" is simply the ordinary common sense of social existence, not a rarefied ethical principle more honored in the breach than in the observance. The fact that the real world generally prefers "do unto others before they do unto you" is difficult for many reasonable people to accept. I know and am very fond of such altruistic rationalists. They may be the salt of the earth, but they are utopians in a distinctly dystopian world. More power to them, but their illusions are not for the likes of me.

Some other rationalists, the Franz Kafkas among us, suffer their rationality to be engulfed by the nightmarish irrationality of the world. I do not recommend this as a direction to which one should become reconciled either.

Rationalists need to understand how the world really works. It does not now, it never has, and it never will function in anything like the reasonable, orderly, and humane fashion that is dear to the hearts and minds of many rationalists. But our society does function, and the majority of people probably think that, on the whole, it functions pretty well. My own view is not that sanguine. I suggest that our Western world at present operates close to the edge of dysfunctionality, by a process that I refer to as *structural chaos*. By that I mean the following. Each institution of our society has some often loose organization or structure, determined by procedures, credentials for membership, methods and apparatus, and so forth. Within this structure, however, most of these institutions perform in a largely unplanned and essentially unregulated manner, which maximizes individual actions taken in a largely disorganized fashion. The faith is that out of this structural chaos there will eventually emerge a serviceable pattern and that, in any case, intensive planning and regulation of society's operations and institutions are simply not feasible and must inevitably fail to deliver the greater good.

In my opinion, the accidental nature of structural chaos is not an accident. While it is assuredly not the sublime expression of human character and intelligence that the champions of present-day society maintain, structural chaos is a pragmatic and necessary accommodation to two crucial aspects of the current human condition: first, to the demands made by the extraordinary complexity and constant restlessness of our civilization, and, second, to the limited capacities of the human species for altruism and rational intelligence (see Chapters 1 and 6). With respect to its ever-growing complexity, our industrial and postindustrial societies have become increasingly resistant to rational overall control. The rapidity and the transilient nature of innovation in our times make it exceedingly difficult just to keep abreast of, let alone direct, change. This contemporary lack of control is manifested in many unfortunate guises: in massive overpopulation, in severe environmental degradation, in the exhaustion of natural resources, in the forced extinction of biological species, to name but a few. As for rational intelligence and altruism, it is much less difficult these days for an individual to devise a single technological innovation (to which, along with making money, much of our intelligence is currently being devoted) than it is to join with others in the society to exercise responsible control over the whole range of its operations—and to do so for the greater, rather than the individual, good. Altruism is too often sucked down into the bog of selfishness and materialism.

Structural chaos, however, exacts a huge price from society. One of its gravest consequences is the enormous wastefulness and inefficiency it generates in the society's operations. When they are not simply ignored, such defects are justified by the claim that they are absolutely necessary in order to maximize progress. Planning and regulation, it is firmly believed by many thinkers, might appear to be less wasteful than structural chaos in the short run, but in the end they would fail to produce as successful an outcome. We must ask, however: to what extent are such thoughts determined by objective analysis or by the self-interest of these thinkers?

To examine these matters in greater detail, I consider three institutions of modern society—scientific research and how it is conducted, the capitalist economic system, and political democracy—with respect to the structural chaos that I believe is intrinsic to their operations. (I could as well take on many other of our institutions, such as our educational system, technology, religion, popular culture; but these three should serve my purpose.) The first of the three I know something about, having practiced it most of my adult life. I maintain not only that structural chaos characterizes the operations of scientific research as we currently carry it out but also that, surprisingly, such chaos is inseparable from its ultimate success in the creation of new knowledge.

THE CONDUCT
OF SCIENTIFIC RESEARCH

In previous chapters, we have dwelt extensively on modern scientific knowledge but have not had much occasion to take heed of how scientific research is actually conducted or of the scientists who participate in it. I referred briefly in Chapter 3 to the belief that scientific knowledge is the ultimate refined product of a complex and often disorderly process; the scientific knowledge attained finally transcends this all-too-human behavior. In this section, however, it is the process itself that is the focus of our attention.

Modern scientific research deals with understanding the universe we live in, the nature of the cosmos, the material basis of life, and other such fundamental questions. Science is distinct from technology, which constitutes our efforts to manipulate our surroundings, including living things, with the goal of achieving greater control of the environment and a more comfortable existence for human beings. Science is not about making money. Research that is about making money is not science, but rather technology. I will not discuss modern technology; I consider here only science and, in particular, research in modern biological science.

The way this research is generally conducted in the United States (closely paralleled in structural features, if different in details, in other industrialized nations) is by individuals, located in academic or research institutions, who usually must satisfy certain criteria of education, experience, and demonstrated scientific ability to be so employed. These individuals generally apply for research funds from government agencies such as the National Institutes of Health or the National Science Foundation, submitting specific research proposals that are reviewed and evaluated by groups of their scientific peers. These factors constitute the structural organization of the conduct of research. Within this structure, however, individual scientists are free to choose their own research programs, subject to the constraints of limited research funds and of their proposed research being judged suitable by their peers. Without going into the merits and defects of the peer review system as it currently operates, it does ensure that administrative types with only a limited knowledge of science have little say in what science gets done. The fact is that there is no (at least, not yet) overall planning of the biological research enterprise. There is no body of either scientists or administrators that meets regularly to decide which specific research areas in biology should be encouraged and which should not be. (The one exception is the Human Genome Project.) Neither is there any significant regulation of the science apart from that indirectly involved in the granting of the funds essential to carry out the research on an individual basis—or, rarely, as in the case of human cloning, when society regards a research area as too threatening.

This mode of operation fits the prescriptions of structural chaos. The engine that runs the scientific research enterprise is fueled by largely independent individual contributions that are not pre-planned or directed by any collective body. What the individual independent research worker chooses to do is what gets done. Among the consequences of this structural chaos, however, are enormous wastefulness and inefficiencies, as well as serious distortions, in the operation of the research enterprise. Our better scientists are extremely reluctant to acknowledge this situation because they fear, probably correctly, that it will be misunderstood by the general public, including politicians who are innocent of any adequate understanding of science or the scientific enterprise.

The simple facts, however, are these. The majority of research scientists are merely competent and hardly innovative, and, as a result, much of the research that gets done and published is redundant and inconsequential. A few years ago, the Institute for Scientific Information (ISI), which has computerized scientific publications and the citations made to them by other scientists, revealed that nearly half of the scientific papers published in scientific journals were never once cited in papers written by other scientists in the five years following publication.[1] This revelation evoked a storm of fury in the scientific establishment. While the absence of citation on rare occasions may mean that a study is so good that it is ignored by other scientists because it is well in advance of its time, the more general inference is that much published (let alone unpublished) scientific research is useless to any other scientist and is simply embalmed on library shelves. The ISI was attacked, however, for malicious distortion and worse, in the best tradition of killing the messenger bearing bad tidings. Actually, the situation is even worse than it appears, because the citation of a scientific paper in other publications is by no means proof of the excellence of the cited work. Generally, it attests merely to the work's immediate relevance, which, however, might often be only marginal.

These reflections, and my own long experience in science, lead me to conclude that there is simply not enough talent in that part of the human species that gravitates to scientific research to allow more than a minority of scientists to do the truly original work that advances scientific knowledge. The rest, for the most part, embellish the work of that minority, carrying out its obvious extensions, or doing the same things in a slightly different way, or on a different but related system. Much of this embellishment is in fact cited by other scientists, and some of it is even marginally useful, if not significantly new, information. But a lot of it is sheer waste motion. Furthermore, the lack of original research talent among a large part of the scientific establishment helps to create a "bandwagon" effect. Certain subdisciplines fostered by the studies of a few competent scientists become fashionable and are pursued to the neglect of other areas of science that are equally worthy of investigation. In modern biology, for example, marine biology (with its enormous variety of unusual living forms) and plant biology (at least until recently, when the commercial applications of plant genetics became recognized) have unjustifiably been scientific backwaters compared, for example, with mammalian biology. This distortion is also reinforced by the orientation toward human health of the main source of financial support of the biological sciences, the National Institutes of Health.

Why is this situation generally ignored, or at least tolerated, by the scientific establishment? Of course, it is in the interests of the majority of scientists to ignore it, for otherwise many of them might be disqualified from research and restricted to teaching science or might be otherwise employed. But that is not the crux of the matter. The principal justification for permitting structural chaos to rule the operations of the scientific research enterprise, despite its attendant waste, inefficiency, and distortion, is the widespread recognition that it is impossible for any scientist or group of scientists, no matter how talented, to provide adequate overall planning for future scientific research. It is in the very nature of truly groundbreaking and innovative science that its future developments are unpredictable and may come from unexpected sources. Everyone knows the story of the young physicist who was forced to become a functionary in a Swiss patent office because he was not considered bright enough by his professors to be offered one of the junior university positions available. In the time he could spare from conscientiously analyzing patent applications, he produced five masterpieces of theoretical physics in the year 1905, going on to become one of the two or three acknowledged scientific geniuses in history.

The problems with weeding out waste and inefficiency in the conduct of scientific research include, first, the enormous effort and expense that would be required to do it and, second, and more important, that it might be done by very ordinary human beings, with the real danger that a few of the most beautiful flowers like Albert Einstein would be rooted out along with the weeds. These are powerful arguments, and they make me subscribe unequivocally to the cause of structural chaos in the operations of scientific research. It would require an unheard-of level of superior intelligence to carry out satisfactory long-term planning of the scientific research enterprise; lacking that, structural chaos is the only alternative.

The further and very important practical justification for tolerating structural chaos in the management of scientific research is that, by God, it works! For one thing, even the support of less-than-first-rate research has an indirect but crucial benefit to society. Such research serves to attract and keep interested the large mass of competent teachers needed to help teach university and college science curricula. That is no small consideration. Furthermore, the new knowledge pouring out of the more productive scientific laboratories and offices continues to be ever more magnificent and a glory of the human race. Despite, or perhaps because of, the structural chaos, those scientists who are capable of doing original research are by and large funded. As we concluded earlier, the eventual outcome of this often vertiginous process, after the completion of many experiments that confirm certain ideas and disprove others, is a refined piece of knowledge that transcends the process itself. If some considerable waste and inefficiency are inevitable accompaniments of the acquisition of that treasure of knowledge, so be it. Don't mess with success.

CAPITALISM

What I have just said about the conduct of modern scientific research, in its unspoken and pragmatic consent to human realities, accords the concept of structural chaos a significance that is unexpected and even disturbing. After all, *chaos* is generally used as a pejorative term. To elevate chaos to a principle of action, as I have done in connection with the operations of scientific research, appears to give it a dignity it otherwise does not usually possess. The next question is whether other institutions of society also operate via structural chaos and, if so, whether, as in the case of scientific research, that chaos is important if not essential to their success, given the nature of our society and of the human condition. We turn now to the institutions of capitalism and the capitalist economy in our society.[2]

But first a disclaimer and a few qualifying remarks. I am not a student of economics. I recognize that modern economics is a far more complex realm than even that of the natural sciences and is inextricably bound up in politics, technology, and human nature. I therefore freely acknowledge that my treatment of capitalist economics, particularly as brief a treatment as this one must be, may to some be considered superficial. Nevertheless, let us take a deep breath and plunge in.

I suggest that free market capitalism is a kind of economic organization that conforms to the criteria of structural chaos. The means of production, including heavy industry, are generally in private hands, with a few exceptions in which state ownership of railroads and energy resources is maintained. Individuals, as isolated entrepreneurs, perceive a demand that they can supply. They then set up businesses and industrial enterprises, usually funded initially with money borrowed from banks or occasionally from a government agency. If they can sell their products or services at a profit, they will prosper, create employment opportunities, and benefit not only themselves but society as a whole. Unfettered competition and a free market are supposed to ensure low prices and high quality.

So goes the theory. The practice, however, is not so salubrious for society. Free market capitalism involves an incredible waste of human and natural resources and often great inequities in the distribution of the wealth generated by the system. These and other deplorable problems arise because the sole real objective, and measure of success, in modern capitalism is to obtain the maximum short-term profit for the individual entrepreneurs and their financial backers. The needs of society as a whole are not significant considerations, except in times of war. As a consequence, all kinds of pernicious anti-social practices are too often employed and countenanced to maximize profits as rapidly as possible. The rivers and air are polluted by industrial wastes, irreplaceable natural resources are devoured with little regard to the future, and the labor force is treated not so much as a body of fellow citizens but rather as a costly and often recalcitrant mechanical resource. Therefore, outsourcing, the bypassing of local laborers in favor of much cheaper workers in underdeveloped countries, and the substitution of robots and automation for humans wherever possible in our manufacturing plants are among the practices that are justified in a capitalist economy even though they may be inimical to the interests and welfare of many of its citizens. The drive for efficiency (read: greater profits) has led to the extensive mechanization of agriculture in the United States, the consolidation of farms into immense acreages, and the nearly complete elimination of the country's small individual farmers in this past century. We insist that Japan do the same to its small-scale rice farmers, who cannot compete in a free market with the rice produced by large and mechanized American farms; but the Japanese, being more concerned than we about maintaining their traditions and culture, have so far resisted abandoning their rice farmers to the free trade market, to our great indignation.

With American factory workers increasingly thrown out of industrial work by outsourcing and automation and American farmers thrown off the land, being unable to compete with agribusiness farming, what is supposed to happen to the great body of physical laborers in this country? Most of them are not suited to desk jobs, and many will have to enter the service industry to make up the menial majority in the techno-capitalist society. Few of our economic and political leaders seem to be seriously concerned about this potentially paralyzing human problem.

There is also another vexatious issue. American capitalists made the astonishing discovery early in the twentieth century that enormous and unprecedented wealth could be generated by catering intensively to the material comforts and desires of the rapidly growing middle class. In most societies in history, it was the satisfaction of the comforts of the ruling class—the monarchy, the nobility, and some of the clergy—that was a significant source of wealth; but ruling classes were always small in number if not in appetite. The Industrial Revolution, beginning in the late eighteenth century, made the bourgeoisie not only the largest class in the Western world but also fairly prosperous and literate.

The middle class in the United States in this century has been able to purchase not only the necessities of life—decent housing, an adequate diet, suitable clothing, health care—but has been prevailed upon to buy a whole host of nonnecessities, even luxuries, made available by capitalist enterprise. (Of course, being constantly surrounded by luxuries makes one think of them more as necessities.) By now, a family that owns just one automobile confesses to the world that it occupies only a low socioeconomic stratum in our society. Automobiles, recreation vehicles, boats, luxury homes, designer clothes, microwave ovens and frozen foods that eliminate the ordeal of cooking, cell phones, personal computers and access to the Internet, a vast assortment of appliances, radios, TVs, VCRs, and many, many more items have all become household fixtures. Every year or two, the previous incarnation of a luxury item is made obsolete by a new, improved (and more expensive) version. Desires that were previously unknown to the human race are brought to white heat by the advertising industry, promoting items to be purchased on unlimited credit.

These economic activities dedicated to the material comforts of the large middle class are much more immediately profitable to entrepreneurs than are those activities catering to the well-to-do—let alone those directed to the poor, such as the amelioration of the terrible plight of the inner cities or the provision of good low-cost housing, cheap public transportation, or quality public education. Infrastructure maintenance, universal health care, and a host of other vital expenditures for society's benefit also remain largely underfunded in a free market capitalist economy.

The middle classes in the outside world are enchanted by and envious of this materialistic paradise. Any economic system that will not or cannot aspire to this kind of mindless hedonism starts out at a great comparative disadvantage in the modern world.

Another source of substantial wealth in our economy is a powerful and highly technical military industry that is in private hands. In the name of national security and American hegemony, we support for ourselves, and sell to our friends and allies, an elaborate and very expensive military arsenal. We spend about $25 billion a year just to maintain our nuclear weapons in peacetime. The United States is the largest military supplier in the world today, even with the Cold War over. This may not always be in our best long-term security interests, but it surely makes huge profits for some.

This brings us to a crucial question: How does one judge the success of an economic system? In a democratic society, the major criterion should presumably be whether it provides the greatest good for the greatest number. (The definition of "good" is, of course, a key issue here, as is the time frame to be considered— for the current decade or generation only, or for future decades and generations as well?) In order to determine whether the greatest good is indeed served by free market capitalism compared to any other economic system, we would have to undertake complex cost-benefit analyses that would take into account the often hidden and terrible costs of the operations of the capitalist economy to public health and welfare, to the environment, and to future generations. This is never done by capitalism's partisans. Nor should we overlook the extent to which a strictly profit-motivated and materialist economy strains the moral and cultural fabric of our society. Perhaps we should be more concerned about the fate of Sodom than of Saddam, but none of our political candidates is likely to adopt that as his or her campaign slogan.

Let us now turn to briefly consider possible national economic systems other than free market capitalism. The alternatives to capitalism in the modern world are various forms of a planned economy, which differ from one another in the extent to which the means of production and distribution are under state control or are in private hands. With the fall of the Soviet Union and the abandonment by its successor states of the communist economic system, with its near-total state control, in favor of free market capitalism, it has become the conventional wisdom of the West that no planned economy is workable and that the intrinsic superiority of free market capitalism in the modern world has been clearly demonstrated. Never mind that over 20 percent of the world's population still practices a planned economy. Never mind that Russia in 1917 was for a variety of reasons the least favorable nation in Europe for the introduction of a proletarian-administered communist economy—and that despite this, in a little more than 30 years, the USSR became the second most powerful industrial and military colossus in the world, having survived the loss of 11 million of its people, mostly peasants, to starvation during Stalin's ruthless collectivization of agriculture in the late 1920s and early 1930s and having endured the further loss of 27 million people and untold havoc and destruction in successfully resisting the mighty Nazi war machine.[3] Thus a more objective inquiry than the conventional one needs to be made into the relative virtues and defects of a planned economy.

What does a planned economy profess to offer in the modern world? Presumably, it would be decided by agreement among appropriately chosen leaders of the society to provide products and services considered most important for the welfare and happiness of its citizens, over the short and long term, and to choose the most economical, humane, and environmentally conservative ways to obtain these products and services. The population would be apportioned to such activities according to their preferences and appropriately trained, or retrained. The predatory instincts of those who, in a capitalist economy, prey on the society and practice malign neglect of the less fortunate would be kept under society's control. This all sounds great! What, then, is the problem?

Unfortunately, planned economies have a number of immense difficulties. I will deal briefly with only a few of the most intractable. One is that economics is not now and never has been a securely predictive science, dismal or otherwise. Karl Marx was a great economist, with many brilliant insights, but he nevertheless was not much at prognostication. He did not foresee, for example, the actions that were ultimately taken to save capitalism in the industrial world, particularly the creation of the welfare state. Modern economic systems are tremendously complex interaction networks (see Chapter 8) and are not amenable to the reductionist methods of the natural sciences. Capable economic experts therefore often completely disagree, whereas natural scientists are able to reach an eventual consensus. As a result, much uncertainty and confusion are generally involved in the design and detailed operation of a successful planned economy, particularly if it is carried out by politicians, many of whom may be economic blunderers.

Furthermore, planning an economy means predicting the economic future, which also means predicting and accommodating to the technological future that will greatly influence the economy. But the technological future is no more competently predictable than is the scientific future. Just as the unpredictability of science militates against successful planning of scientific research, the uncertainty about the coming decades of technological change makes intelligent planning of a modern economy extremely tenuous. The USSR could certainly compete with the United States for a while, imitating or even exceeding some of its heavy industry, especially while the United States was suffering through the Great Depression. A succession of Five-Year Plans wrought a tremendous industrial revolution in the USSR, but they were imposed at tremendous social cost. (In the process, by the way, the Soviet Union became one of the industrial world's worst environmental polluters, not the kind of thing one might hope for from a well-planned economy.) However, in the post-industrial age, when its huge factories ultimately became obsolescent, the USSR could not respond quickly enough to the need to change. Adaptability to unanticipated and rapid changes is an essential requirement of a modern economic system. Free market capitalism does not actively promote such adaptability; instead, it passively relies on the profit incentive to encourage individual entrepreneurs to introduce and develop new and profitable industries or to adjust relatively rapidly to altered economic and technological conditions. Those industries that innovate, or adjust to innovation, prosper; those that do not, go under, and their employees find other jobs or join the ranks of the un-employed. Economic life marches on.

A second formidable problem for a planned economy is to pro-vide at all levels, from the highest leadership to the ordinary worker, a large enough number of altruistic, intelligent people, who with the utmost dedication, enthusiasm, and selflessness are ready to make the necessary personal sacrifices to establish and operate an effective economy for the greatest good of the great-est number in the society. At the top, the economic complexities and likely fiercely contested views may create a stalemate that can lead to absolute power being seized by a ruthless and megaloma-niacal dictator, as happened by 1929 in the USSR. If a takeover by a Stalin were to be the likely consequence of a command econ-omy, it would be an unacceptable choice to most. And at the bot-tom of the ladder, few people who are hungry and cold are likely to put the needs of the greater society before their own for long. Their genes do not work that way (see Chapter 6).

Lester Thurow, a liberal economist, puts the problem this way: "Socialism was invented...as a remedy to the visible nineteenth century defects of capitalism—widening inequalities, rising un-employment, a growing workforce of castoffs. To cure these de-fects, socialists believed, *it would be possible under socialism to build a new human being—a 'social individual.'*...Communism failed be-cause in practice no one succeeded in creating the new human being. It proved impossible to motivate most human beings to work hard for social objectives for very long."[4] (Italics mine.) And then there is the testimony of Michael Manley, who was the prime minister of Jamaica from 1972 to 1980. A strong advocate of state control of the economy, he changed his mind and became a sup-porter of capitalism, in part because, as he wrote in 1992, "...when one tries to use the state as a major instrument of production, one quickly exhausts the managerial talent that can be mobilized in the name of patriotism. Absent the profit motive, it was truly amazing how few managers one could find that were motivated solely by love of their country, and how quickly these noble souls burned out."[5]

In addition to these inescapable human factors, there are forbidding material obstacles to implementing a newly organized planned economy in today's world. That economy, for example, must generally quickly begin to compete in trade with the capitalist world for the petroleum and other crucial resources it might not possess, to run its industrial development without being suffocated by debts. The planned economy is not permitted to get on its feet slowly unless it can, as the People's Republic of China did for a long time, isolate itself from the world markets. The Chinese relied instead on their vast domestic market and largely retained their inefficient but essential rural agrarian economy (73 percent of the population is still employed in agriculture, compared with less than 2 percent in the United States) while developing an industrial base.

It is entirely possible, therefore, although hardly established by sufficient experience, that over the long term a capitalist economy, for all its many faults, will generally outperform a planned economy on behalf of society. The saving grace of capitalism is that, unlike a planned economy, it does not depend upon a large body of selfless, intelligent people willing to act in concert for the greater good. Capitalism requires only an adequate number of independent entrepreneurs ready to cultivate their self-interest. (Only a handful of technologists/entrepreneurs were responsible for setting in motion the entire computer revolution in the West.

In just a few years, each became enormously wealthy.) This provides the system with adaptability and allows it to accommodate to technological innovation. Some of the benefits then diffuse to others in the society. The possible advantages of capitalism might be increased if it distributed more equitably the enormous wealth that it generates and if it was regulated in greater deference to the public good. One need hardly add, however, that all this does not exactly constitute a ringing endorsement of the structural chaos known as capitalism. I suggest that it simply may not be possible to implement a more rational and less chaotic industrial or post-industrial economic system in the world as it exists today.

But the monstrous vulgarity of capitalist society—particularly as trumpeted by the economic oligarchy's wholly owned subsidiary, the advertising industry—is difficult for an intelligent person to live with. Furthermore, capitalism is sometimes difficult to distinguish from prostitution. Its voluptuous temptations can induce a delirium in weak natures. In our times, these temptations have caught practitioners of even such ministerial professions as medical care, the academy, scientific research, and the law, let alone government, in compromising situations. More seriously, severe problems with capitalism may become manifest in the future. First, as the resources of the planet continue to be exploited with great profligacy, the time will certainly come when increased efficiencies of resource utilization will become mandatory. Whether a free market capitalist economy can remain free and make the profound adjustments required to effect these efficiencies is not clear. Second, the scale of individual kinds of technology has been continually enlarging in the recent past, a pattern that will almost certainly increase in the foreseeable future. Certain kinds of essential technology, such as massive energy production by means other than the extraction and burning of fossil fuels, may first require prodigies of research and development that will not be encouraged in a system that functions by short-term profitability and in any event would be beyond the resources of individual entrepreneurs to develop. At such a stage of technological amplification, cooperation and concerted action may be forced on humanity, and planned national economies may become necessary to civilized survival.

POLITICAL DEMOCRACY

The third societal institution I examine is our democratic form of governance. For a nation to be a political democracy means that it grants universal suffrage to its citizens and is ruled by the decisions of the majority. The alternatives to democracy in modern society are either some type of tightly controlling oligarchy, theocratic or secular, or a dictatorship, benevolent or otherwise. I maintain that democracy as a method of governance represents a kind of structural chaos. Democracies, by their deferral to conflicting interests, find it difficult to carry out any long-term planning and have a hard time following a coherent policy on behalf of the public good. Oligarchies and dictatorships usually have a sense of direction and can impose their plans on a society, although this is often done for the greater benefit of the oligarchs or the dictators rather than for the society as a whole.

Two major theoretical ideas provide the structural scaffold of modern political democracy. One is that all human beings are equal before the law; equal in the rights to life, liberty, and the pursuit of happiness; and equal in the eyes of their Maker. These are fundamentally ethical and religious notions, expressing the equality of the vital spark in each human life. The second idea, which is sometimes considered a corollary of the first, is that all human beings are essentially equally capable, if given the opportunity to be fully informed and to express their talents. This idea, as I noted before, is really a biological rather than an ethical one. The first idea is a noble and honorable one. The second idea is a myth. It has no basis in biological science (see Chapter 6). The first idea, as difficult as it has been to achieve in practice, is the luminous glory of the enduring dream of political democracy. The second idea contributes to the structural chaos that characterizes the modern American practice of democracy.

The myth that the great majority of human beings are intrinsically equally capable has never really been taken seriously by any society throughout history, except our own Western society. It arose during the period of the Enlightenment some two centuries ago. It originated as a response of exhilarating optimism by liberal intellectuals to the triumph of human reason that was represented by the Newtonian synthesis. The Marquis de Condorcet is an exemplary figure of this utopian intellectual tradition. An aristocrat and a famous mathematician, elected to the Académie Française at the age of 39, Condorcet became a staunch early supporter of and active participant in the French Revolution. For this, he was of course pilloried as a traitor to his class. Later, however, when the revolution was taken over by the more bloodthirsty Jacobins, Condorcet's brand of reasonableness and good will went out of fashion, and he went into hiding. Before being hounded to death by his former revolutionary compatriots, and presumably while dodging their knives and bullets, Condorcet wrote a treatise on history that culminated in his vision of the coming perfectibility of the human race! If a movie were ever to be made of

Condorcet's life, it would be a difficult decision whether he should be portrayed by a Laurence Olivier or a Mel Brooks. I have never known whether to laugh or cry over him.

Down to the present day, many intellectuals of an altruistic bent have been partial to this myth of the perfectibility, the intrinsic equality, of most human beings. This faith has not been shaken, even by overwhelming everyday evidence to the contrary. Throughout the world, the explosive growth of fanatical fundamentalist religions and the bloody turmoil created by barbaric ethnic and racial hatreds among former neighbors have once more revealed the irrational and primitive human underpinnings beneath the facade of sophisticated modern society. How these and countless similar horrible excesses of the past century, occurring even in nations with the most highly educated and cultured populations, such as Hitler's Germany, can be reconciled with the perfectibility of human beings escapes me.

On the other hand, the members of the loosely organized but potent economic oligarchy that quietly oversees the governance of American democracy, that screens and funds the candidates for public office, that (very important, though hardly noticed) employs them lucratively after they leave office, that intimidates political dissenters, that manipulates the information media it controls, and that administers profitably to the needs and desires it creates in the general public never have been among those who believed in the equality and perfectibility of humanity. Earlier in the twentieth century, however, people who ran this country appeared to honor an unwritten compact made with the society. Perhaps unnerved by the World Wars and the Great Depression, they generally submitted to treating the American public with some measure of dignity and consideration as if, indeed, all were worthy citizens in a democracy. But in recent years, its nerve restored, the oligarchy has abandoned this compact. Everything is now up for sale. Even life. In this highly pietistic country, a biotechnologist can genetically modify one of God's creations, a living plant or animal, and then claim its exclusive ownership and sell it as private property, without even sharing any of the credit or profits with the Co-Creator. All with hardly any public or ecclesiastical demurral.

The mantra of the 1960s, "make love, not war," has been superseded by today's "make money, not love." In the 1960s and 1970s, the economic oligarchy carefully groomed an affable grade-B movie actor for high political office. At first, his mental vacuity was a national joke, but the image makers behind him soon changed that perception; and in 1980 he was elected president of the United States. Promptly, he and his Congressional helpers gutted the regulatory and tax laws to ensure the further enrichment of the oligarchy for which he fronted. As a consequence, *90 percent of all the gains in male incomes in the decade of the 1980s went to the top 1 percent of the male workforce.*[6] (With you, I too find that hard to believe, but it is not a misprint.) Furthermore, for the first time since records have been kept, in the 1970s and 1980s a majority of American workers saw their real wages reduced at the same time that the real per capita GDP increased. Corporate downsizing, outsourcing, and the American worker's fear of being fired now dominate our economic landscape.

In politics, sloganeering has replaced discourse; sound bites and calculated distortions have superseded political analysis. There are only a few significant critics of our system in Congress. A good many of our best members of Congress, fed up with our dysfunctional system, have quit public service in recent years. Presidents and presidential aides suffer remarkable lapses of memory and stonewall Congress or, if they deem it necessary, deliberately lie to it with equanimity. Taxation, which was once on a par only with Death, has now been raised in the public consciousness to a still higher level of apocalypse, thereby paralyzing any semblance of responsible governance. State governments raise funds by sponsoring lotteries that soak the poor. (Is this supposed to encourage a higher standard of morality and the work ethic among them?) Gambling on Indian reservations has become Sitting Bull's and Geronimo's revenge on their former enemies.

Mass culture is dominated by professional sports, which has been inflated so far beyond all reasonable bounds that it has now taken over from religion the role of opiate of the people. In the popular media, in television and motion pictures, sex and berserk violence have now been thrust to the fore, on the obvious grounds that the oligarchy that owns the media makes greater profits from distributing mindless mayhem than from intelligent entertainment. In affluent neighborhoods, suburbanites venture forth from their barricaded bastions and resolutely wrestle their $50,000 4-wheel-drive mini-tanks all the way to the supermarket. Meanwhile, only a few miles away, but seemingly on another planet, loom the desolate and teeming inner cities. Once the fertile proving grounds of new immigrant generations, they have now been effectively cordoned off from the rest of society and serve as battlegrounds of a drug-engendered civil war between the jobless poor and the unemployed poor, battlegrounds that our president may visit, surrounded by an army of bodyguards, to give a speech honoring the battle casualties on Memorial Day. Elementary public education, which in my youth was the ship of hope for me and other children of those less well off in our society, has now been cast adrift by the oligarchy in a sea of neglect and indifference.

If this overall condition of our political democracy doesn't serve as almost a definition of structural chaos, it is hard to imagine what would. The sheer degradation of moral standards, the enormous waste of potential talent, the subversion of the future that accompanies such chaos represent a terrible price to pay for our democracy. How can it be justified?

Very simply. Given the realities of the human condition, everything else would very probably be much worse.

In modern times, no closely controlled political society, oligarchical or dictatorial, has ever been successful for very long, if success is measured by the overall happiness and well-being of its citizens. The twentieth century has seen many such experiments. The total subordination and murderous rampages inflicted by communist, fascist, and Nazi dictators and the vicious thugs they often elevated to the governing elite have permanently ruled out any responsible advocacy of such forms of governance. In a theocracy, if you happen to pick your nose or cross your eyes when the Holy Imam passes by, you are liable to be instantly decapitated. That is no way to live, either. Democracy is the least repressive and least intolerant form of governance; this is of particular and crucial importance to all rationalists and nonconformists.

In 1939, on the eve of the Second World War, with the object of rallying the British people to oppose Hitler's impending invasion and to defend their political democracy, E. M. Forster was asked to deliver an address over the BBC. It was a very realistic speech. As published, it was entitled *Two Cheers for Democracy.* Exactly.[7]

• • •

A person of rational persuasion and good will is hard pressed to understand the irrationality of modern advanced society and the absurdity and wastefulness that appear to characterize much of its activities. My explanation is that the operations of the society are of necessity chaotic, that chaos is built into the structure of these operations and is not accidental. That is what I mean by structural chaos. Individuals make decisions and carry out actions that are usually neither coordinated nor planned by any higher-level body or authority in the society. I argue that this structural chaos is an implicit accommodation to two inescapable facts: first, the bewildering and ever more rapidly increasing complexity of our society's institutions, and, second, the limited supply of human beings with the required combination of altruism and high intelligence to conduct a potentially more satisfactory planned, coherent, and less wasteful operation of these institutions. To illustrate these ideas, I have examined the structural chaos that I believe is built into three key areas of modern society: the conduct of scientific research, the capitalist economic system, and political democracy. (I must note, however, that not all of our institutions operate chaotically. Take the symphony orchestra, for example. [I refer here to its music making, not to its economic viability in our democratic culture.] An orchestra, the epitome of rationality and talent, requires the immersion of each individual's talents and interests into the operation of the whole. Is there a lesson to be learned here?)

The case of the conduct of modern scientific research is particularly interesting and unexpected. Science is, after all, that institution beyond all others where rationality should reign supreme; and yet I contend that its operations are not only structurally chaotic but necessarily so in order to maximize its effectiveness, given the complexity and unpredictability of much scientific discovery and the limited distribution of scientific talent. The saving grace for science is that the human limitations of the research process are ultimately transcended, and meaningful knowledge can be extracted from it. Could this prominence of structural chaos also be true of institutions and operations of our society that are intrinsically much less rational than science? I suggest that this is at least plausibly so, for the institutions of a capitalist economy and of political democracy. The case that these two institutions operate via structural chaos is rather easily made. What is less obvious is whether structural chaos represents, from the point of view of the greater good, the least ineffective way for the economy and the political governance of modern society to function. I suggest, however reluctantly, that this may well be true.

I now return to the questions with which this chapter started: How can rationalists effectively engage with the real world? How can they contribute to a saner society and to a more tolerable future? It seems to me that the first order of business is to dispense with outworn myths and dogmas. Rationalists have no difficulty in dismissing the myths that, for example, capitalism as an economic system and democracy as a form of political governance are the highest and most nearly perfect forms of rational human conduct, as it is obvious to any thinking person that these institutions currently operate in ways that are often grossly irrational, mindless, and immoral. But altruistic rationalists also need to give up the myth of the perfectibility of humankind, beatific and alluring as it might be. They have to realize that while the institutions of our society are deeply flawed, they may nevertheless be the least ineffective ways to accomplish the greater good, given the facts, and not the myths, of the human condition.

That realization can have profound consequences for how rationalists approach the real world. Intelligent altruists who are unhappy with the institutions of modern society must come to realize that a frontal assault on these institutions is not practicable, given the minority status of rationality in modern society. If, however, they accept the idea that of necessity the world functions through structural chaos, it may lead them to adopt particular courses of action that they might otherwise think unpromising. Instead of abandoning these structurally chaotic institutions and devoting themselves to the support of a radically different and more rationally organized planned economy or to a modernized Platonic republic, they might concentrate on more realistic aims; namely, finding the means to minimize the waste and control the inequities of our present institutions and to reduce the severe burdens these create for the society and for the future. In the process, significant stepwise progress may be achieved in increasing the role of rationality in the operations of the world.

A lesson of history is that the key to such progress in the intrusion of reason into human affairs lies in the fact that on particular and not infrequent occasions the irrational world becomes vulnerable to a significant pulse of change. This vulnerability arises when the uncontrolled greed and sometimes just plain stupidity of the ruling class create an intolerable crisis. It took the catastrophe of the Great Depression, for example, to open the door to the New Deal and its program for increased economic justice for the middle and lower classes in our society.

Such an unusual opportunity to force a profound change for the better in the operations of our political democracy currently exists. Our present government is utterly dominated by the economic oligarchy, because election to high office is entirely contingent upon a candidate raising and spending vast sums of privately supplied money for television advertising and electioneering. The American public is apparently finally becoming fed up with the blatant corruption involved in such fund raising and is ready to see the process reformed. The ethical standards of political democracy in this country will continue to sprawl in the gutter until candidates for all significant elective offices of government are strictly limited to the use of publicly provided campaign funds. Reform, however, is in the hands of a Congress that makes a show of dealing with the problem and passes an occasional bill that is full of Lincoln Tunnel-size loopholes. Public opinion must be effectively aroused and channeled to force the enactment of meaningful reform. This one action could accomplish enormous benefits. It would encourage first-rate candidates, including many intelligent altruists, to run for public office, candidates who cannot or will not run under the present unfavorable and degrading conditions. Such candidates, replacing the sycophants of the economic oligarchy and the bigots of the religious right who so often occupy these offices now, could alone introduce an almost unimaginable revival and elevation of the operations of our democratic government.

An elected government that was finally beholden to the interests of the entire society could then adjust the operations of our capitalist economy, if it is the system that we have no choice but to run with, to ensure greater fairness and the benefit of all. Such a government would make it easier for entrepreneurs to invest more in socially productive technologies and would discourage the nonproductive and harmful ways that many entrepreneurs now use to make a short-term killing. Both these objectives can be met by private enterprise if the government employs the appropriate tax policies. The enormous sums of money required to reverse the many decades of neglect of the inner cities might then finally be raised. A good democratic government with responsible leaders might encourage us to temper our national obsessions with greed and personal comforts and promote public discourse to address the real problems of our world, instead of largely ignoring them as we do now.

The message is this: rational people of good will must often find it frustrating and repellant to witness and participate in the irrational and often predatory operations of the real world. It seems obvious to many of them that we would all be better off if the best and the brightest were elected to govern. They feel in their bones that it is possible to conceive of different kinds of institutions that would work much more effectively than the ones we have: such institutions could be better organized, more efficient, more equitable, and less destructive. However, institutions operate within real, not imaginary, societies. Institutions above all are limited by the values of the society and by the people available to run them. I have tried to make the case that, given the human condition, many of our institutions may be the least unsuitable alternatives among those that have been suggested or tried, at least at this time in our history. If that is acceptable, then rational people of good will may decide to shelve their efforts to discard and replace our present institutions and learn to cope with the structural chaos that is intrinsic to them. Once they recognize this, they can then devote themselves to finding the means to reduce significantly the many burdens such chaotic operations place upon all of us.

Rationalists need to promote in the public domain an understanding of the nature of aging and death that is biologically and socially realistic. They must also advance the pragmatic program for survival that derives from even a modest understanding of modern biology. That science, as I have tried to make clear, can shed considerable light on the social, political, legal, and, above all, the technological-economic activities of our society—not only to help make them more reasonable and efficient sets of operations but, much more critical, to ensure the very survival of the inhabitants of the planet in the future. Make no mistake about this: our descendants are at great risk if our present massive and mindless assault on the biosphere continues largely unabated.

But accommodating to the real world while also trying to bring sense and reason to it are not the only salient responsibilities of rationalists. These represent the immediate obligations they owe to their society, but they also owe abiding obligations to themselves and to the future of the best and brightest in human culture. As an individual rationalist, whether in the scientific tradition of an Albert Einstein, the literary and intellectual tradition of a Paul Valéry, or the spiritual tradition of an Albert Schweitzer, one must nourish one's inner light of reason, however benighted the real world may be. A rationalist must cherish his or her rare gift of reason. Accommodation to the real world, with its indifference, at best, or hostility, at worst, to the muted sounds of reason, should not entail any abandonment of the fullest exercise of one's individual rationality. That exercise is a ceremony of innocence in an often depraved world. Even if the planet we live on were indeed "the insane asylum of the solar system,"[8] rationalists do not have to compromise their sanity in order to survive, and even to enjoy themselves, while they are among the inmates. Only in this way will intellectual ferment and the sublimity of the human mind be maintained and augmented for the generations to come. In an irrational world becoming ever more irrational, as Paul Valéry asked some sixty years ago, "What will become of independence of mind, independence in the pursuit of knowledge, independence of feeling? What will become of intellectual freedom?"[9] It is the essential role of the rationalist by his or her own life's work to help ensure that these questions will be relieved of their anguish and that the life of the mind will continue on its magnificent journey.

APPENDIX A

THE STRUCTURES AND FUNCTIONS
OF PROTEIN MOLECULES

As indicated in the text of this book, proteins mediate most of the functions of the cell, with each kind of protein characterized by a particular linear chain of connected amino acids, as encoded in its corresponding stretch of DNA. This sequence of amino acids determines the folding of each kind of protein chain into a unique three-dimensional arrangement in the milieu of a cell. This structure is the most stable one for that particular sequence in a water solution. As a representative example of the protein enzymes, consider the protein carboxypeptidase A (shown in Figure A). It is a chain of 307 amino acids, whose backbone is folded up as indicated in the figure—a structure that was determined experimentally by X-ray crystallographic analysis. A principal purpose of this complex structure is to generate and stabilize a region near the surface of the molecule that is designated the "active site" (shown in the middle left portion of the figure). The active site is a bowl-shaped depression lined with certain specific amino acid residues, as indicated. This site is the region of the protein where the chemical reaction mediated by the enzyme takes

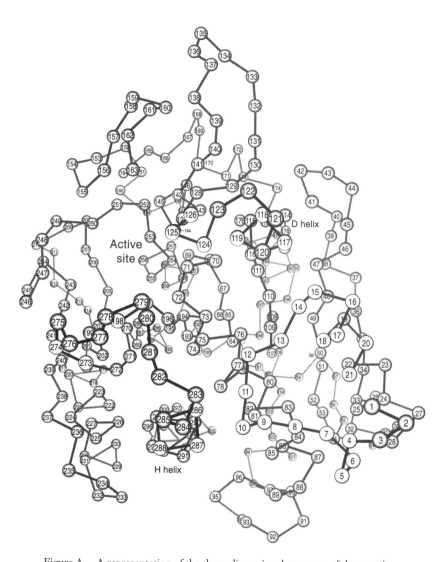

Figure A. A representation of the three-dimensional structure of the protein enzyme carboxypeptidase A. To appreciate the complexity of the structure, follow the convolutions of the chain of amino acids from residue 1 (lower right) to the last numbered residue, 305 (lower center). Some of the residues are folded into characteristic helices, so-called α-helices (labeled D, upper right; and H, lower center). Reproduced with minor modification, and with permission from the estate of Irving Geis, from Richard E. Dickerson and Irving Geis, *The Structure and Action of Proteins* (New York: Harper and Row, 1969).

place. Every protein enzyme has its unique active site, with its unique function, that is generated by the unique folding of its specific chain of amino acids. The chemical rules that determine the folding are only partially understood at the present time. See E. O. Wilson et al., *Life on Earth*, 2d ed. (Sunderland, Mass.: Sinauer, 1978), pp. 88–92, for more details about carboxypeptidase A structure and function.

THE GENETIC CODE

The genetic code consists of the 64 different sets of triplets (codons) of the four nucleotide bases uracil (U), cytosine (C), adenine (A), and guanine (G). (The code is based on messenger RNA, in which the base uracil replaces the base thymine [the T in Figure 1, page 49] of DNA.) The table presented here in Figure B gives the name of the amino acid that is encoded by each triplet codon. For example, the triplet CAG has the first letter C, the second A, and the third G; as read from the table, the amino acid that CAG specifies is glutamine. Since there are 64 codons but only 20 amino acids to encode, most of the amino acids are encoded by any one of several (two to six) different triplet codons. In fact, only the amino acids methionine and tryptophan have just one codon. The methionine codon AUG in certain situations acts as a signal to start a protein chain, and any one of the three codons UAA, UAG, and UGA are signals to end the chain, as it is linked together one amino acid after the other by the action of the messenger RNA passing through the ribosome.

The identical genetic code exists in virtually all forms of present-day

FIRST LETTER	SECOND LETTER				THIRD LETTER
	U	C	A	G	
U	PHENYLALANINE	SERINE	TYROSINE	CYSTEINE	U
	PHENYLALANINE	SERINE	TYROSINE	CYSTEINE	C
	LEUCINE	SERINE	(END CHAIN)	(END CHAIN)	A
	LEUCINE	SERINE	(END CHAIN)	TRYPTOPHAN	G
C	LEUCINE	PROLINE	HISTIDINE	ARGININE	U
	LEUCINE	PROLINE	HISTIDINE	ARGININE	C
	LEUCINE	PROLINE	GLUTAMINE	ARGININE	A
	LEUCINE	PROLINE	GLUTAMINE	ARGININE	G
A	ISOLEUCINE	THREONINE	ASPARAGINE	SERINE	U
	ISOLEUCINE	THREONINE	ASPARAGINE	SERINE	C
	ISOLEUCINE	THREONINE	LYSINE	ARGININE	A
	METHIONINE	THREONINE	LYSINE	ARGININE	G
G	VALINE	ALANINE	ASPARTIC ACID	GLYCINE	U
	VALINE	ALANINE	ASPARTIC ACID	GLYCINE	C
	VALINE	ALANINE	GLUTAMIC ACID	GLYCINE	A
	VALINE	ALANINE	GLUTAMIC ACID	GLYCINE	G

Figure B. The genetic code.

life on Earth, from bacteria to human beings. This is one of the profound kinds of evidence supporting Darwinian evolution. On the practical side, the conservation of the code permits a human protein to be made inside bacteria if the appropriate human messenger RNA is inserted into the bacterial cell.

MITOSIS (ASEXUAL REPRODUCTION)

In mitosis, a parental cell divides into two cells that possess exactly the same genes as the parental cell. The process by which this is accomplished is presented in a highly schematized fashion in Figure C. For our purposes, we further simplify things by considering a cell with only two pairs of chromosomes. (A human cell has 23 pairs.) Most of the time a cell is not dividing; the process of division takes only around 30 minutes. The onset of division first involves the replication of the DNA in the parental cell (step 1 in Figure C), which produces two copies of each chromosome that remain attached to each other, as shown in stage *a* of the figure. In step 2, each pair of copies is then lined up along the mid-region of the cell (see stage *b*), tethered by microtubules, which are threads made of a special protein called tubulin. The microtubules are attached at one end to the middle of each copy of the chromosomes, and at the other end to structures called spindle poles, located at opposite poles of the cell.

In step 3, the two copies of each chromosome are detached from each other, and a mechano-chemical process acting on the microtubules pulls

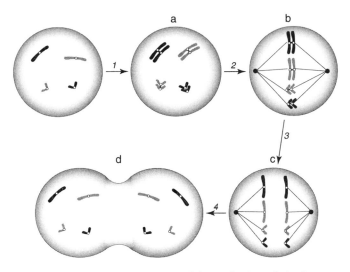

Figure C.   A simplified schematic view of the mechanism of mitosis.

one of each pair of chromosomes to opposite poles of the cell, as shown in stage *c*. In the final step, the cell undergoes division into two halves (see stage *d*), producing two cells that are identical genetically to each other and to the parental cell. In the mitosis of a human cell, all 23 pairs of chromosomes line up along the mid-region of the cell, as in stage *b*, and are segregated equally into the two daughter cells, as shown here.

MEIOSIS (SEXUAL REPRODUCTION)

Whereas most cells in the body divide by mitosis, only a special group of cells (the germ-line precursor cells) is set aside to undergo meiosis, in both males and females of the species. The purpose of meiosis is to produce sperm cells in the male and egg cells in the female that have two distinctive characteristics: 1) whereas the precursor cells in any one individual are all genetically identical, the sperm or egg cells derived from them are genetically diverse; and 2) the sperm or egg cells contain only half the number of chromosomes that the precursor cells contain. For example, human sperm or egg cells contain 23 chromosomes, although the precursor cells contain 23 *pairs* of chromosomes. This halving of the number of chromosomes occurs so that upon subsequent fertilization (fusion) of an egg cell with a sperm cell, the *fertilized* egg cell that results will again have 23 *pairs* of chromosomes, one of each pair derived from the sperm cell, and the other from the egg cell.

Meiosis occurs in two separate stages, known as Meiosis I and Meiosis II, which are represented in highly schematic outline in Figure D. In

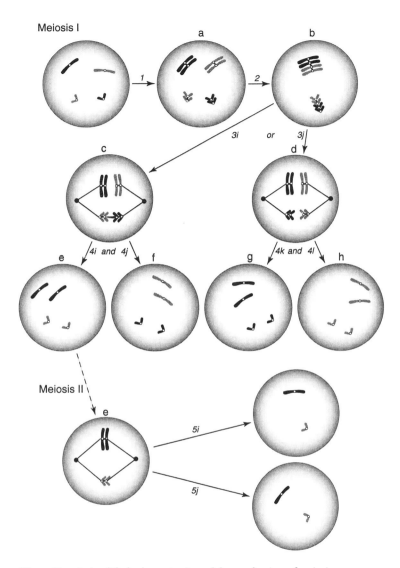

Figure D.   A simplified schematic view of the mechanism of meiosis.

the figure, I have simplified the process by considering a parental precursor cell containing only two pairs of chromosomes.

MEIOSIS I

As in mitosis, the first step is replication of the DNA in the precursor cell and the production of a pair of attached copies of each chromosome (stage *a*). Now, however, a process occurs that is unique to meiosis: the two pairs (four copies) of each kind of chromosome become attached to one another to form a tetrad (stage *b*). Following this step, when all the tetrads are lined up along the mid-region of the cell, an interesting situation arises. When there are two kinds of chromosomes, this lining up can occur in either of two alternative ways (either *c* or *d*). In the next steps, each tetrad is cleaved in two, the two halves are segregated to the spindle poles, and cell division occurs. This process can result in four *genetically different* cells (see *e, f, g*, and *h*), each with a pair of copies of both chromosomes. The number of genetically diverse cells that are possible when the cell contains *n* different chromosome pairs is 2^n. It is therefore the staggeringly large number 2^{23} for humans. This is the end of Meiosis I, and these cells, which are the immediate precursors of the sperm and egg cells, are often stored in the body until required for the next stage of meiosis.

MEIOSIS II

In this process, each of the precursor cells (*e, f, g*, and *h*), without any further DNA replication or chromosome duplication, undergoes chromosome segregation and cell division to produce two identical cells called gametes: the sperm cells in the male and the egg cells in the female. Figure D shows this process for the precursor cell in stage *e*. Note that each gamete contains only one copy of each chromosome.

UNEQUAL CROSSING-OVER

Crossing-over (or recombination) is a relatively frequent event that occurs during the tetrad stage of Meiosis I. (See stage *b* of Figure D in the preceding appendix.) Crossing-over involves cleavage of the DNA chains in both of two adjacent chromosomes and a chemical reannealing of crossed-over segments. Most of the time, such crossing-over is equal: that is, the cleavages occur at exactly homologous positions of the two strands of DNA. Sometimes, however, the crossing-over is unequal, when the cleavages occur at different positions on the two chains (as indicated by

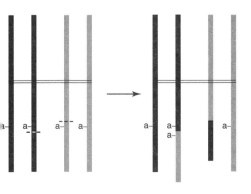

Figure E.   Unequal crossing-over that can occur during the tetrad stage of Meiosis I.

the dashed lines in Figure E, left, occurring in one chromosome below the gene *a*, and in the other above the gene *a*). Crossing-over now produces two chromosomes of the tetrad (see Figure E, right), in which one chromosome has two copies of the gene *a*, and the other has none. These recombined chromosomes then proceed normally through the remainder of Meiosis I and II. Some of the gametes will then contain a chromosome with two *a* genes, others a chromosome containing none. This process is referred to in the text as gene duplication.

MINNESOTA TWIN STUDIES

The scientific findings of the Minnesota Center are collected in two articles: A. Tellegen et al., "Personality Similarity in Twins Reared Apart and Together," *Journal of Personality and Social Psychology* 54 (1988): 1031–1039; and T.J. Bouchard, Jr., et al., "Sources of Human Psychological Differences: The Minnesota Study of Twins Reared Apart," *Science* 250 (1990): 223–228. The two tables of data abstracted from these studies are presented here. The data are given as correlation coefficients between the two twins of a pair, averaged over the number of pairs studied. A correlation coefficient of 1.0 represents a perfect correlation; a coefficient of 0.0 represents a complete absence of correlation. (For randomly chosen pairs of individuals, the correlation coefficients were always close to 0.0.)

The results in Table 1 are for identical twins only. Table 2 additionally includes data for fraternal twins who were reared apart or together. For most of the personality variables, the correlation values between fraternal twins were, first, roughly half that for identical twins and, second,

TABLE I   MINNESOTA TWIN STUDIES

Variable	Identical Twins Reared Apart		Identical Twins Reared Together		Ratio R_A / R_T
	$R_A{}^\dagger$	*Number of Pairs*	$R_T{}^\dagger$	*Number of Pairs*	
Fingerprint pattern	0.97	54	0.96	274	1.01
Height	0.86	56	0.93	274	0.93
Weight	0.73	56	0.83	274	0.88
Mental ability					
WAIS IQ—full scale	0.69	48	0.88	40	0.78
WAIS IQ—verbal	0.64	48	0.88	40	0.73
WAIS IQ—					
performance	0.71	48	0.79	40	0.90
Raven, M-H composite	0.78	42	0.76	37	1.03
Personality variables					
Average MPQ scales	0.50	44	0.49	217	1.02
Average CPI scales	0.48	38	0.49	99	0.98
Psychological interests					
Average SCII scales	0.39	52	0.48	116	0.81
Average CPI scales	0.40	40	0.49	376	0.82
Social attitudes					
Religiosity	0.49	31	0.51	458	0.96
Social attitude scale	0.34	42	0.28	421	1.21
MPQ traditionalism					
scale	0.53	44	0.50	217	1.06

SOURCE: Data from T.J. Bouchard, Jr., et al., "Sources of Human Psychological Differences: The Minnesota Study of Twins Reared Apart," *Science* 250 (1990): 223–228.
    † R values are the correlation coefficients of the responses between each twin of a pair, averaged over all pairs. The subscript A refers to twins reared apart from an early age; the subscript T refers to twins reared together.

were not substantially different whether the twins were reared apart or together. Both facts accord with the conclusion that genetic factors play a more important role in determining these personality traits than does the environment. (Fraternal twins have only 50 percent of their genes in common, only half the amount of identical twins.) However, certain traits give anomalously low correlation between fraternal twins, whether reared apart or together: these include achievement, aggression, and control.

TABLE 2   MINNESOTA TWIN STUDIES:
CORRELATION COEFFICIENTS[†]

Variable	Identical Twins Reared Apart	Fraternal Twins Reared Apart	Identical Twins Reared Together	Fraternal Twins Reared Together
Well-being	.48	.18	.58	.23
Social potency	.56	.27	.65	.08
Achievement	.36	.07	.51	.13
Social closeness	.29	.30	.57	.24
Stress reaction	.61	.27	.52	.24
Alienation	.48	.18	.55	.38
Aggression	.46	.06	.43	.14
Control	.50	.03	.41	−.06
Harm avoidance	.49	.24	.55	.17
Traditionalism	.53	.39	.50	.47
Absorption	.61	.21	.49	.41

SOURCE: A. Tellegen et al., "Personality Similarity in Twins Reared Apart and To-gether," *Journal of Personality and Social Psychology* 54 (1988): 1031–1039.

[†] The correlation coefficients are averages of 44, 27, 217, and 114 sets of twins for columns 2, 3, 4, and 5 of the table, respectively. The variables listed represent the breakdown into the several categories of the Multiple Personality Questionnaire (MPQ) that were averaged and listed in Table 1.

Regarding the two environments in which the members of a pair of twins were reared apart, detailed studies showed that overall there was no significant correlation between the two milieus that could account for the absence of a detectable environmental influence on the twins' behaviors.

CAIN AND ABEL: THE SEQUEL

Interpreters of the Bible have long recognized that the story of Cain and Abel has a deeper meaning than it might at first appear. It is really a fable about a critical turn in the history of humanity: the triumph of agriculture over the previous hunter-gatherer culture. For most of the several million years of human history, human beings led a nomadic existence, subsisting for food on what nature barely provided, supplemented later on by domesticating a few animals such as sheep and goats. As recently as 10,000 years ago, however, the invention of agriculture revolutionized the human condition. The cultivation of a few cereals and other plant species for the first time made food available in dependable surplus. This liberated the enormous powers of human intelligence to an extent previously unrealized, which soon led to the development of written languages, the rise of great religions, and the quest for increased knowledge and understanding of the natural world. The growth of great cities and civilizations inexorably followed. No more important transformation in the pattern of human life has ever occurred.

The story of Cain and Abel, the first two sons of Adam and Eve, mythologizes this agricultural revolution. Abel, *the keeper of sheep*, represents the traditional rough-and-ready nomad with his domesticated flock, whereas Cain, *a tiller of the ground*, represents the more settled, and more neurotic, newer breed, the agriculturist. To honor the Lord God, Cain brings an *offering of the fruit of the ground*, and Abel brings *of the firstlings of his flock and of the fat thereof*. Not worried about cholesterol, *the Lord had respect unto Abel and to his offering, but unto Cain and his offering He had no respect*. When Cain becomes distraught by this rejection, the Lord says to Cain, "*Why art thou wroth?*" Just keep up the good work, bar sin from your door, and you will come out alright. And besides, *unto thee shall be his [Abel's] desire, and thou shalt rule over him*. Thus, God tells Cain that despite his temporary setback, he will ultimately triumph and rule over Abel. The fable assures us that agricultural society will supplant the nomadic culture in due time.

Well, we all know what happened next. Cain, after all, was only human. He was also probably not terribly bright, thinking that he could fool the Lord. Anyway, for his murderous transgression, Cain is doubly punished. *When thou tillest the ground, it shall not henceforth yield unto thee her strength*, the Lord tells him. *A fugitive and a vagabond shalt thou be in the earth.* Life on the farm will be hard and unrelenting, and drought and locusts will take their terrible toll. But to protect Cain from being slain by others for his crime, *the Lord set a mark upon Cain, lest any finding him should kill him*.

Now, 10,000 years later, we are on the threshold of another agricultural revolution, perhaps even of greater magnitude than the first. The scientific understanding of genetics that has been acquired in the past 50 years has brought forth a new technology, bioengineering. It has become feasible to implant new or altered genetic information into plant species, raising incredible possibilities for increased efficiencies of agricultural productivity. Cereals and other plant foods will eventually be grown without the need for fertilizers, will be made extraordinarily efficient in capturing the sun's energy, will be rendered resistant to insect destruction and to diseases, and will flourish even under the harshest environmental conditions. A new era in food production is therefore just around the corner. And it is thus high time to bring the Cain and Abel fable up to date.

You remember that some time after Abel's demise, *Adam knew his wife again; and she bare a son and called his name Seth: For God, said she, hath appointed me another seed instead of Abel, whom Cain slew.*

Now Seth...

ITEMS FOR THE SEQUEL

Seth Adamson, a first-generation American.

His father, Adam, and his mother, Eve, were immigrants to America who had been forcibly deported from their native land with nothing but the clothes on their backs.

Once in America, Adam and Eve settled in Massachusetts and had two sons, Cain and Abel, who didn't get along too well. Cain was a truck farmer in western Massachusetts, and Abel was a butcher in a nearby town. Abel died under peculiar circumstances that the family never talked about. There is a rumor that shortly after Abel's death, Cain awoke one day with a tattoo on his arm that showed a snake with an apple in its mouth and the words "Don't tread on me."

Later, Seth was born. After an uneventful childhood, Seth matriculated in Molecular and Cell Biology at Harvard, and then, being more interested in making money than in doing scientific research, he joined a biotechnology firm outside Boston, called Sell Biology, Inc. He gradually worked his way up to CEO.

Sell Biology made a big investment in a bioengineered tomato. They named it TomatoE (for "tomato-engineered"), little realizing that this would subsequently cause a great deal of confusion among immature minds about the proper spelling of tomato. TomatoE had engineered into it a set of remarkable properties that made it commercially valuable. It was disease-, frost-, and drought-resistant, and it did not require artificial fertilizer to grow, even in the most barren of soils. Furthermore, it grew to full size but remained green and hard indefinitely without spoiling. However, if brought to 100 degrees Centigrade for three minutes, it turned from green to brilliant red, and from hard to juicy ripe. It was terrific for storage and shipping compared to the conventional tomato.

In order to promote TomatoE, Seth decided to exhibit his product at the Massachusetts State Fair, not knowing that his brother Cain was simultaneously submitting some of the organically grown tomatoes from his farm. Unfortunately for Seth, the Judge presiding over the competition didn't even know how to boil water, and so TomatoE remained green and hard. The Judge therefore awarded First Prize for tomatoes to Cain. This made Seth terribly wroth—in fact, overwroth.

The Judge, seeing that Seth was about to launch a veritable philippic of wroth against him, said, "What's the big deal? All that TomatoE needs is a little more engineering and a big publicity campaign. Look, after a few more years, you'll have it all over your brother Cain, so relax."

But Seth was not soothed; in sooth, Seth seethed. Constrained from taking physical vengeance on Cain by the Lord's mark on him, Seth employed the generalist education he had received at Harvard. (He had minored in Economics.) After a few inquiries, he found out which bank held the mortgage to Cain's farm and arranged to buy the bank. Seth then foreclosed on his brother's farm. So Cain and his family were forced from the land, became vagabonds, and never grew organic tomatoes again.

TomatoE became a great hit with the American consumer and then captured the world market. Seth became a multibillionaire, served as honorary chairman of the American Family Association, was asked to join the Harvard Board of Overseers, and lived happily ever after.

Chorus: "*Plus ça change, plus c'est la même chose.*"

NOTES

CHAPTER 1

1. George Gallup, Jr., *Public Opinion 1982* (Wilmington, Del.: Scholarly Resources, 1983).

2. J. D. Miller, *The American People and Science Policy* (New York: Pergamon, 1983).

CHAPTER 2

1. The ancient Chinese, contrary to Westerners in this as in almost everything else, had a different myth of the Creation of the Universe and the human race. According to this myth, the Universe began as an egg. After a time, the egg split in two, the top becoming the Heavens and the bottom the Earth. Pan Ku, or Phan Ku, the progenitor of humans, came out of the broken egg; and after 18,000 years, he died. He then split into a number of convertible parts. His head became the sun and the moon, his blood the

rivers and oceans, his hair the plants and forests, his sweat the rain, his breath the winds, and his voice the thunder. Lastly, his fleas became the ancestors of humankind! So much for the centrality of Man in the cosmos.

2. A. F. C. Wallace, *Religion: An Anthropological View* (New York: Random House, 1966), p. 3. This surprisingly large figure of 100,000 is based on several assumptions: that religion began as early as the Neanderthals, who we know had developed careful burial rituals; that a thousand or more distinct and generally isolated human societies have existed at all times since then, each with its own religion; and that these religions have changed into culturally distinct entities at least every thousand years.

CHAPTER 3

1. In particular, more information about Galileo's magnificent work and writings can be found in Stillman Drake's books: *Discoveries and Opinions of Galileo* (New York: Doubleday, 1957); and *Galileo at Work: His Scientific Biography* (Chicago: University of Chicago Press, 1978). It is difficult for us moderns to realize, for example, that there were no mechanical methods for measuring short intervals of time when Galileo conducted his careful experiments of the laws of motion. In fact, Galileo used his pulse for the purpose. The pendulum clock was not invented until later in the seventeenth century.

2. Copernicus wrote in partial justification of his heliocentric model of the solar system: "But in the midst of all stands the sun. For who could in this most beautiful temple place this lamp in another or better place than that from which it can illuminate the whole? Which some not unsuitably call the light of the world, others the soul or the ruler" (quoted in A. C. Crombie, *Augustine to Galileo* [London: Mercury Books, 1964], vol. 2, p. 174). That is superb scientific intuition expressed in humanistic terms (see p. 160).

3. The best among the political left have an abiding concern for the dignity and the welfare of common people. They would like to believe

in the perfectibility of humanity, and they thus view genetic determinism with great suspicion. This sometimes, however, makes them victims of charlatans like Trofim Lysenko. Lysenko used his position as the scientific leader of Soviet agriculture in the USSR in the 1930s and 1940s to promote the long-discredited idea that hereditary traits can be acquired by appropriate stimuli from the environment rather than only by genetic mutation and transmission. He convinced his boss, that eminent biologist Joseph Stalin, to expunge the science of genetics from the USSR. The effects on Soviet agriculture were disastrous, and it took two decades before Soviet genetics recovered from his influence. Scientific truth is no more the servant of political or social dogmas than of religious ones.

CHAPTER 4

1. Irreversible thermodynamics constitutes the mathematical principles that govern systems undergoing change, by delineating the kinds of changes that are allowed; see I. Prigogine and I. Stengers, *Order Out of Chaos* (New York: Bantam Books, 1984). Reversible thermodynamics, on the other hand, mathematically defines the conditions for the state of equilibrium, where no net change occurs in a system.

2. Every nook and cranny of life abounds with chemical wonders. For example, in almost all photosynthetic organisms, the molecule that nature has evolved for the absorption of light's energy is called chlorophyll. Its special chemical structure allows chlorophyll to capture (absorb) both blue and red light from the sun's spectrum, and their energies are then used for photosynthesis. Chlorophyll, however, does not absorb green light, which is therefore all reflected into our eyes. This is why we see chlorophyll, and all plant life containing it, as green. And so arises the verdant beauty of the world.

3. Ignoramuses, including some Hee-Haw U.S. Senators, have relished the public ridicule of supposedly wasteful and irrelevant government-supported research with project titles like "The Sex Life of the Sea

Urchin," not knowing that, because of evolutionary relationships, the information that can be obtained from such studies is often highly relevant to human biology.

4. The genes set off a regulated program of the production of specific proteins at specific places and times in the developing embryo. These proteins then carry out the processes of development. This program is not set in concrete, however. It can be altered by certain changes introduced into the embryo, such as drugs (as in the case of the thalidomide catastrophe); but normally, in the absence of such perturbations, the undisturbed program almost always yields the same body plan. For further details, see, for example, W. McGinnis and M. Kuziora, "The Molecular Architects of Body Design," *Scientific American* 270, no. 2 (1994): 58–66.

5. Erwin Schrödinger, *What Is Life?* (Cambridge: Cambridge University Press, 1967).

CHAPTER 5

1. Lewis Thomas, "On the Science and Technology of Medicine," *Proceedings of the American Academy of Arts and Sciences* 117 (1988): 299–316.

2. An extended analysis is presented in M. R. Rose, *Evolutionary Biology of Aging* (New York: Oxford University Press, 1994).

3. See Rose, *Evolutionary Biology of Aging.*

4. In his book *The Future of Capitalism* (New York: Morrow, 1996), Lester Thurow takes dead aim at the complacency with which Western societies generally view the economic consequences of their aging populations. He writes: "A new class of people is being created. For the first time in human history, our societies will have a very large group [projected to be at least 20 percent of the U.S. population by 2025] of economically inactive elderly, affluent voters who require expensive social services such as health care and who depend upon government for much of their income. They are bringing down the social welfare state, destroying government finances, and threatening the investments that all societies need

to make to have a successful future" (p. 96). He then proceeds to provide the facts and statistics to support this alarmist view. Furthermore, no politician who isn't suicidal dares to take on this powerful bloc.

5. V. R. Fricks, "Health Care for the Elderly: How Much? Who Will Pay for It?" *Health Affairs* 18 (1999): 11–21.

CHAPTER 6

1. For example, Aristotle, in "Nicomachean Ethics," says, "All admit that in a certain sense the several kinds of character are bestowed by nature. Justice, a tendency to Temperance, Courage, and the other types of character are exhibited from the moment of birth."

2. As Cervantes opined, "Every man is as Heaven made him, and sometimes a great deal worse."

3. For details of these not-so-cuckoo cuckoo behaviors, see R. M. Kilner, D. G. Noble, and N. B. Davies, "Signals of Need in Parent-Offspring Communication and Their Exploitation by the Common Cuckoo," *Nature* 397 (1999): 667–672. Also take a look at the Prologue of William Congreve's play *The Way of the World*, published in 1700.

4. See, for example, R. F. Foelix, *Biology of Spiders* (Cambridge, Mass.: Harvard University Press, 1982); T. H. Savory, *The Spider's Web* (London: Warne, 1952); and P. N. Witt, C. F. Reed, and D. B. Peakall, *A Spider's Web* (Berlin: Springer, 1968).

5. The decisions made by a spider in many stages of a web construction involve making a choice at each stage among multitudes of possibilities. Such choices must be made expeditiously; there is no time for much in the way of trial and error. Question: How are the decision-making processes of the spider distinguishable in kind from what we humans call "thinking"? Can spiders really think? Are they conscious? Most would say no, but on what firm basis? See also p. 68.

6. Two useful guides to modern studies of language structure are N. Chomsky, *Knowledge of Language: Its Nature, Origin, and Use* (New York: Praeger, 1986); and S. Pinker, *The Language Instinct* (New York: Morrow,

1994). For a different view, see J. Elman et al., *Rethinking Innateness: A Connectionist Perspective on Development* (Cambridge, Mass.: MIT Press 1996).

7. One example of an epigenetic difference between two identical twins involves their susceptibility to multiple sclerosis; see U. Utz et al., "Skewed T-Cell Receptor Repertoire in Genetically Identical Twins Correlates with Multiple Sclerosis," *Nature* 364 (1993): 243–247.

8. This conclusion was stated by J. K. Galbraith in *The Affluent Society* (Boston: Houghton Mifflin, 1958), p. 330.

CHAPTER 7

1. See, for example, R. A. Kerr, "Early Life Thrived Despite Earthly Travails," *Science* 284 (1999): 2111–2113.

2. See, for example, S. Yachi and M. Loreau, "Biodiversity and Ecosystem Productivity in a Fluctuating Environment: The Insurance Hypothesis," *Proceedings of the National Academy of Sciences, U.S.A.* 96 (1999): 1463–1468.

3. Although the birth rate in the developed world has decreased significantly, the rate in the underdeveloped world is still too large, relative to the extension of life expectancy, to reduce the rate of growth of the world's total population significantly. Conservative projections are for total population to increase from its current 6 billion to 8.5 billion by 2030 and to 10.4 billion by 2100. (See J. Bongaarts, "Demographic Consequences of Declining Fertility," *Science* 282 [1998]: 419–420.) Compounding the problem is the U.S. resistance (religiously inspired) to providing the underdeveloped world with more effective means of birth control. One result is a great surge in immigration from the underdeveloped world to the United States; this immigration is viewed with great hostility by the same conservatives who fiercely oppose the dissemination of effective birth control.

4. The supply of fresh water is likely to be the first major technological predicament the twenty-first century will encounter; see P. H. Gleick, ed., *Water in Crisis* (New York: Oxford University Press, 1993).

5. In all the current furor about abortion of genetically defective embryos, it is generally not realized by the public that more than 30 percent of developing human embryos are *spontaneously* aborted during normal gestation; if these occur late enough, they are called miscarriages. See, for example, A.J. Wilcox et al., "Time of Implantation of the Conceptus and Loss of Pregnancy," *New England Journal of Medicine* 340 (1999): 1796–1799.

6. One of many useful guides to the effects of technology is B.L. Turner II et al., eds., *The Earth as Transformed by Human Action* (Cambridge: Cambridge University Press, 1993).

CHAPTER 8

1. See, for example, Ernst Mayr, *Toward a New Philosophy of Biology* (Cambridge, Mass.: Harvard University Press, 1988), and many references cited therein.

2. I have, on several other professional occasions, referred to the concept of fixed functionality as *idiocrasy*. It is as idiocrasy that the concept was taken up in some of its philosophical ramifications by A. Stroll; see Stroll, "Ethics Without Principles," in *Wittgenstein and the Philosophy of Culture*, ed. K.S. Johannessen and T. Nordenstam (Vienna: Holder-Picher-Tempsky, 1996).

3. There are many examples of proteins with dual functions that are quite different from each other, and it is likely that in different cellular environments one or the other of the dual functions predominates. For the cognoscenti, a case in point is the enzyme glucose 6-phosphate dehydrogenase from *Leuconostoc mesenteroides*, which can utilize either NAD or NADP as co-factor for the mediation of different chemical reactions, depending on the physiological conditions; see R.D. DeMoss et al., "A Glucose 6-Phosphate Dehydrogenase in *Leuconostoc mesenteroides*," *Journal of Bacteriology* 66 (1953): 10–16. The idea that, very early in evolution, protein enzymes might have been multifunctional and fewer in number is discussed by H. Kacser and R. Beeby, "The Evo-

lution of Catalytic Proteins," *Journal of Molecular Evolution* 20 (1984): 38–51.

4. Alfred North Whitehead, *Science and the Modern World* (New York: Macmillan, 1960).

5. These ideas about fixed and adaptable functionality may also bear on the ongoing debate about artificial intelligence. At issue is whether computers of the future can attain characteristics that are substantially equivalent to human intelligence and perception. Can they ever achieve capacities for thinking and consciousness that are essentially indistinguishable from those of human beings? This is not the place to explore these questions as extensively as they deserve, but one point may be worth making. The basic unit of a computer is an electronic chip. It is, of course, inanimate, a physical and chemical device. As such, a chip exhibits fixed functionality. Once installed, it does one thing only. The basic unit of the brain is a living neuronal cell, which, like most cells, has an adaptable functionality, depending on a history of influences from variable chemical and electrical signals from its surroundings. There is thus a world of difference between the functional potentialities of a neuron and a chip. I believe that these versatile functional features of neurons, as well as their complex interconnections in the brain, are critically implicated in the capacity for thought and consciousness. My intuition is that brains and computers, by virtue of the vastly different natures of their basic units and their connections, are so far apart in complexity and unknown functional potentialities that, along with our meager understanding of how the brain works (pp. 66 and 126), the issue of artificial intelligence is at least premature, if not altogether remote.

6. The importance of long-range interactions on the folding of protein chains is demonstrated experimentally in D. L. Minor, Jr., and P. S. Kim, "Context-Dependent Secondary Structure Formation of a Designed Protein Sequence," *Nature* 380 (1996): 730–734.

7. Useful references regarding parallel computing include the following: "A New Era in Computation," *Proceedings of the American Academy of Arts and Sciences* 121, no. 1 (1992), entire issue; G. S. Almasi and

A. Gottlieb, *Highly Parallel Computing* (Redwood City, Calif.: Benjamin/Cummings, 1994); and R. L. Martino et al., "Parallel Computing in Biomedical Research," *Science* 265 (1994): 902–908.

CHAPTER 9

1. Regarding the limits of reductionism, see K. Mainzer, *Thinking in Complexity: The Complex Dynamics of Matter, Mind, and Mankind* (Berlin: Springer-Verlag, 1994); and J. Cornwell, ed., *Nature's Imagination: The Frontiers of Scientific Vision* (Oxford: Oxford University Press, 1995).

2. An unusual and detailed analysis of the functional connections between our visual perception and our environment was developed by J. J. Gibson in his book *The Ecological Approach to Visual Perception* (Boston: Houghton Mifflin, 1979).

3. E. O. Wilson, *On Human Nature* (Cambridge, Mass.: Harvard University Press, 1978), p. 6.

CHAPTER 10

1. A very useful guide to the concept of complementarity is Gerald Holton, "The Roots of Complementarity," *Proceedings of the American Academy of Arts and Sciences* 117, no. 3 (1988): 151–197.

Although the existence of the wave-particle duality is not in dispute, its physical basis is still under investigation: see S. Durr et al., "Origin of Quantum-Mechanical Complementarity Probed by a 'Which-Way' Experiment in an Atom Interferometer," *Nature* 395 (1998): 33–37.

2. See, for example, Nils Bohr, *Atomic Physics and Human Knowledge* (New York: Wiley, 1958).

3. R. H. Tawney, *Religion and the Rise of Capitalism* (London: Pelican, 1938), pp. 103–104.

4. C. P. Snow, *The Two Cultures and the Scientific Revolution* (New York: Cambridge University Press, 1959).

CHAPTER 11

1. E. Garfield, "I Had a Dream...About Uncitedness," *The Scientist* 12 (1998): 10.

2. From reading this chapter, one is unlikely to come away with the notion that I am a great admirer of the modern practice of capitalism. In the past, though, from around the tenth to the fifteenth centuries in the West, much about early capitalism was admirable. The rise of the middle class that fostered capitalism reinvented commerce in the West and created new and more widely distributed wealth. This commerce and affluence undermined the feudal system and started the West on its long journey to democracy. We owe a lot to capitalism's pioneers.

3. A fair and objective assessment of the economic policies of the Soviet Union can be found in Alec Nove, *An Economic History of the USSR, 1917–1991*, 3d ed. (London: Penguin Books, 1992).

4. Thurow, *The Future of Capitalism*, p. 4.

5. Michael Manley, "Adam Smith Was Right," *New Perspectives Quarterly* 9, no. 3 (1992): 46–51.

6. Thurow, *The Future of Capitalism*, p. 21.

7. E. M. Forster, *Two Cheers for Democracy* (New York: Harcourt Brace, 1957).

8. Several distinguished figures have considered this possibility. The quotation is from Sydney and Beatrice Webb's 1924 book *The Decay of Capitalist Civilization* (Freeport, N.Y.: Books for Libraries Press, 1969). Albert Einstein, in a letter from Berlin to his close friend Michele Besso during the war year 1917, wrote: "I begin to feel comfortable amid the present insane tumult.... Why should one not be able to live contentedly as a member of the service personnel in the lunatic asylum? After all, one respects the lunatics as the ones for whom the building in which one lives exists."

9. Paul Valéry, *History and Politics* (New York: Pantheon, 1962), p. 146.

INDEX

64, 69, 74, 120, 122, 129,
146–48, 227n3; reductionist
techniques in, 142; theory of
relativity, 37
planned economies: benefits of,
181–82; disadvantages of, 182–
85
politics, as dysfunctional, 189–91,
195–96
popular governance, 2
predator-prey relationships, 107
predictions: economic, 182–84;
of protein structure, 137–39;
scientific basis for, 31
Prime Mover, of Aristotle,
27–28
Prometheus, 7
proteins: active sites, 201–3; diversity of, 125; fixed functionality
of, 123–26, 129, 139, 227n3;
functions of, 45, 201–3; interaction networks of, 137–38; structure of, 43–45, 123–24, 137–39,
201–3; turnover of, 72–74
Ptolemy, 28, 29, 34

quintessence, defined, 22

rationality/rationalists: altruism
and, 7; attributes of, 4–5; defined, 3; ethics of, 157–59; as genetically determined, 5–6, 104;
in history, 23; intelligence and,
6–7; as minority, 5–6, 7, 195;
relating to irrational world, 9–
10, 153, 167–99; role in human
affairs, 150, 157–58, 165–66,
194–99; societal distrust of, 7–
8; understanding of universe,
147; views on religion, 17–18

Reagan, Ronald, genetic potential
of, 87
reality, perception of, 143–45
recombination, 59–60, 211–12
reductionist scientific approach: as
cornerstone of modern science,
24, 124, 141–42; to economics,
182; interaction networks and,
137; systems amenable to study
by, 123, 125–26, 133–35, 139,
142
religions: capitalism and, 158; conditioning instilled by, 98, 152;
death and, 18, 71–72; distrust of
knowledge by, 7, 19, 23, 39–40;
diversity of, 16–17; ethics of, 18,
158–60; evolution theories of,
6, 15–16, 41, 52, 53, 146–47;
irrational nature of, 4–5; needs
addressed by, 18–19, 147, 152,
160; negative attributes of, 19–
20, 166, 189; role in early science, 22–23, 25, 153; role in
politics, 196
reproduction: asexual, 54–56, 69,
206–7; to compensate for death,
74; sexual, 56–58, 69, 98–99, 110,
208–12
research: on cancer, 131; on evolution, 223–24n3; on human behavior, 93–96, 149, 213–15; intuition as tool, 30, 164, 222n2;
public distrust of, 223–24n3; on
social problems, 131–35; structural chaos in, 170–76
resource utilization, in capitalist
economic systems, 177–78,
186–87
rhodopsin, function of, 44
ribosomes, function of, 49, 204–5

Compositor: Impressions
Text: 10/15 Janson
Display: Janson
Printer and binder: Rose Printing